Catch the Spirit of Love

GEORGE SWEETING

While this book is designed for your personal reading enjoyment, it is also intended for group study. A Leader's Guide with Victor Multiuse Transparency Masters is available from your local bookstore or from the publisher.

VICTOR BOOKS a division of SP Publications, Inc.
WHEATON. ILLINOIS 60187

Offices also in
Whitby, Ontario, Canada
Amersham-on-the-Hill, Bucks, England

Most of the Scripture quotations in this book are from the *King James Version.* Other quotations are from the *New American Standard Bible* (NASB), © 1960, 1962, 1963, 1968, 1971, 1972, 1973, 1975, 1977 by The Lockman Foundation, LaHabra, California; and *The New Testament in Modern English,* © J. B. Phillips, 1958, The Macmillan Company. Used by permission.

Recommended Dewey Decimal Classification: 248.4
 Suggested Subject Headings: LOVE (THEOLOGY); CHRISTIAN LIFE

Library of Congress Catalog Card Number: 82-062434
ISBN: 0-88207-108-4

To my loving wife,
HILDA MARGARET SWEETING,
whose life and patience have
been sources of constant
inspiration to me

CONTENTS

The World We Live In

1

"The whole world lies in the power of the evil one".
1 John 5:19, NASB

Tradition tells of the farewell message of the aged Apostle John to his first-century congregation. He challenged them to love one another, as he had often done before.

"We've heard that," they responded. "Give us a *new* commandment." John paused thoughtfully and then deliberately stated, "A new commandment I give unto you, that ye love one another" (John 13:34).

The Apostle John had no commandment that could equal in importance the command to love others. As far as John was concerned, everything worthwhile in life was wrapped up in one big bundle of love—for God and people!

Selfishness Motivates Our World
Shocking as it may seem, the world we live in rejects this approach. Instead of love for God and others, selfishness pre-

dominates. A study of books, magazines, and newspapers reveals that the majority of people are indeed "looking out for number one." The recurring themes are, "What's in it for me?" "Do unto others *before* they do unto you." "You only go around once, so grab all the gusto you can." Undoubtedly, you can think of other phrases and songs that convey this obsession with self.

Many news stories reflect undisguised selfishness and greed:

NEW YORK, NEW YORK—A violent storm knocked out powerlines July 13 . . . resulting in a 25-hour blackout marked by widespread looting and violence.

The final cost of the blackout, including damage to property, the city's bills for overtime pay for policemen, and losses to business and people, was estimated at $310 million.

WASHINGTON, D.C.—Once they were among the highest elected officials in the land. Yesterday, the six men known as the Abscam defendants were simply convicted felons about to be sentenced for their crimes. All have been found guilty of accepting bribes from FBI agents posing as Arab sheiks.

CHICAGO, ILLINOIS—All bundled up in her winter coat and mittens, Laura Bruce had sat impatiently in her living room as she waited for her sister to go out to play. There was a knock at the door and Laura's mother, who was decorating the Christmas tree, went to answer it.

Laura had jumped out of her chair to join her mother as she opened the door. Christine Bruce asked twice what the man standing there wanted. His only reply was to point a sawed-off shotgun inside the home. The mother was able to duck out of the way, but a blast of shotgun fire hit Laura. . . . The impact hurled the girl backward until she fell under the Christmas tree. Her father, William, ran to her and held her in his arms as she lay dying. "Daddy, it hurts," is the last thing he remembers his little girl saying. The intruder took some money and fled.

I have several file folders of other stories reflecting the kind of world in which we live.

Ultimately, those who are motivated by self-interest realize that they have leaned the ladder of their life against the wrong wall, resulting in disappointment, defeat, and in some cases, desperation.

In the Metropolitan Museum of Art in New York, you will find a bust to the memory of short story writer Edgar Allen Poe. These telling words are inscribed:

"Great in genius, unhappy in life, wretched in death."

The note of disappointment and despair is characteristic of many, because life lived on the physical plane alone is incomplete and therefore unsatisfying.

What's the Point?

Recently I read excerpts from a fascinating book titled *American Averages* (Fiensiber and Mead, Doubleday, 1980). Some of the happenings were intriguing and even amusing, while others were discouraging and tragic. For example, on an average day in America—

438 immigrants become United States citizens;

41 million people go to school, kindergarten through graduate school;

28 mailmen are bitten by dogs;

motorists pay $4,036,000 in tolls;

10,930,000 cows are milked;

8 children swallow toys and are taken to emergency rooms;

4,109 people parachute from airplanes for the fun of it;

each of us, on average, produces nearly 6 pounds of garbage;

people drink 90 million cans of beer;

people smoke 1.6 billion cigarettes;

2,740 children run away from home;

88 million people watch prime time television programs;

2,740 teenagers become pregnant;

5,962 couples wed, and before the sun sets, 2,986 divorce;

someone is raped every 8 minutes, someone is murdered every 27 minutes, and someone is robbed every 78 seconds;

a burglar strikes every 10 seconds, and a car is stolen every 33 seconds.

That is the kind of world we live in.

Sooner or later, all of us must ask, "Is life worth all the problems? What is life for? What is my primary motivation? What makes me tick? What really *matters* in life? Is there more to life than just looking out for myself?" These are difficult questions, but they must be asked and carefully answered.

It is said that when comedian Woody Allen was asked what made life worth living, he listed five things:

1. Groucho Marx
2. The second movement of Mozart's "Jupiter Symphony"
3. Louie Armstrong's recording of the "Potato Head Blues"
4. Flaubert's, "A Sentimental Education"
5. Cezanne's, "Still Life of Apples and Pears"

But surely life is more than Groucho Marx and the "Potato Head Blues," isn't it?

A Life-changing Question

Questions about what is important in life are not new; people have been asking them for centuries. One day a lawyer came to

Jesus and asked, "'Master, which is the great commandment in the Law?' Jesus said unto him, 'Thou shalt love the Lord thy God with all thy heart, and with all thy soul, and with all thy mind. This is the first and great commandment. And the second is like unto it. Thou shalt love thy neighbor as thyself. On these two commandments hang all the Law and the Prophets'" (Matt. 22:36-40).

The question asked of Jesus was not trivial. In fact, it was an all-important question: "Which is *the great* commandment in the Law?" (v. 36) To take seriously the answer to that question could change one's life.

It is significant that this question was not asked of an average, run-of-the-mill person. Rather, it was asked of the only Person truly qualified to give an adequate answer. In Christ "are hidden all the treasures of wisdom and knowledge" (Col. 2:3, NASB).

Jesus shocked the lawyer by stating that to love God with all one's heart, soul and mind is the *first* and *great* commandment, and that to love *others* is the second. "On these two commandments hang all the Law and the Prophets" (Matt. 22:40). The Pharisees were devastated. Jesus was saying that unless they loved God fully, and mankind as well, all their good deeds and sacrifices were wasted efforts. "All our righteousness are as filthy rags" (Isa. 64:6).

The greatest thing in the world is to be a channel of God's love. This truth was taught in Old Testament times by Moses (Deut. 6:5), and it was affirmed by Jesus (Matt. 22:35-40). The Apostle Paul also stated this truth so simply that even the youngest could understand. To the believers in Corinth he wrote, "But now abide faith, hope, love, these three; but the greatest of these is love" (1 Cor. 13:13, NASB). What is the greatest thing in all the world? Loving God and loving people. Always remember this: GOD LOVES PEOPLE and so must we.

This Is Life Eternal

As we have seen, the primary motivation of the majority of people in our world is self. We're told it's a dog-eat-dog world. We are urged to "make it while we're hot" because we may not have another chance.

Some insist that, in this production-centered, commodity-greedy world, they would starve to death if they followed the great commandment of Scripture. They insist that the way of love is incompatible with the nitty-gritty of making a living. Are they right?

It is my conviction that loving God and others is the only sane way to a full and meaningful life. You have already observed that the sacred Scriptures support this conviction.

The Book of Genesis states that the world God created was *good*. Repeatedly, the Bible says, "it was good" and Genesis 1:31 affirms that "it was very good."

The world God created was also *orderly*. It revealed pattern and design. In addition, the world God created displayed *abundance* (Gen. 1:20-22). It teemed with a profusion of life. Creation exploded with variety. But the world in which we live is contrary to the world God created.

Aldous Huxley, feeling this nausea of our world, wrote: "What we are looking for in some way is getting beyond our vomit—beyond this piddling twopenny and halfpenny personality."

Instead of order, we see chaos. Instead of abundance, we experience hunger, poverty and desperate needs.

None of us can go back to Eden, but because of Jesus Christ we can choose to live above this present evil world. We can choose to live God's life now.

It has been said that man can live about 40 days without food, about three days without water, and about eight minutes without air . . . but only about one second without HOPE.

The starting point which leads to becoming a loving person is found in the truth of John 17:3: "And this is life eternal, that they might know Thee the only true God, and Jesus Christ, whom Thou hast sent."

Jesus said, "I am come that they might have life, and that they might have it more abundantly" (John 10:10). He also said, "These things have I spoken unto you, that My joy might remain in you, and that your joy might be full" (John 15:11).

Life for some is success. No price appears too great to pay to be successful. Life for others is money. Others are driven by power and still others by pleasure. But what is life for you?

Have you committed yourself to God through faith in Jesus Christ?

One day "doubting Thomas" said to Jesus, "How can we know the way?" (John 14:5) "Jesus saith unto him, 'I am the way, the truth, and the life; no man cometh unto the Father, but by Me'" (John 14:6).

Jesus is the way to the Father and to a joy-filled, abundant life. The following prayer may help you reach the decision to know Jesus:

"Lord Jesus, I confess my personal need of forgiveness for all my sins. I also confess that Jesus Christ, Your Son, died on the cross for me. I want You to turn me around from my own selfish way and put me on Your way. Forgive my sins right now and receive me into Your family. In Jesus' name. Amen."

Coming to know Jesus Christ is the first step toward a meaningful, abundant life, but only the first. We must be willing to evaluate our lives and allow Him to make the changes necessary for us to truly follow Him in love. Are we motivated primarily by self-interest? Have we leaned the ladder of life against the wrong wall? What place does the first and great commandment have in our lives? Are we willing to be channels of love to God, to our families, and to the rest of our world?

What Is Love?

2

"Herein is love, not that we loved God, but that He loved us, and sent His Son to be the propitiation for our sins".

1 John 4:10

There was a time in my life when I was very uncomfortable with the subject of God's love. I recoiled from what some have called "a sloppy agape." I thought that God's love was a convenient cop-out for a spineless, gutless kind of faith.

My response might be partially explained by my Scottish background. My parents were godly, caring people whom I highly honored and deeply loved. They were not, however, given to excessive emotion. I never saw my father cry. He told us that he had forgotten how to cry. And though Mother suffered deeply at times, she would quietly maintain, "We Scots don't wear our feelings on our sleeves."

As a child I was not only an immigrant but also afflicted with a full head of gorgeous curls. The combination of curly hair and being an immigrant child quickly taught me the art of self-defense. Occasionally, when I was in need of courage, my dear mother would softly say, "Laddie, the blood of the covenanters is in our veins." After hearing that, I was ready to take on the whole neighborhood. It was important to me to be strong, and I saw little value in something as "soft" as love.

Love Defined

I have since discovered that I was not alone in my understanding of love. Few people seem to have a clear idea of what it is. The word *love* has been used to describe so many things other than divine love. Sometimes the word *love* is used to mean the intoxicating emotions of romance (and what a marvelous experience that is!). The same word is also used to describe lust, the desire for simple gratification of the flesh. At times the word *love* is used simply to indicate preference: "I just love blueberry pancakes!"

The so-called new morality and situation ethics have compounded the confusion by telling us that there are no absolutes anymore except "love," and whatever is done in "love" must be right.

I reject that concept of love. God's love is pure, holy, and changeless. It cannot be altered and/or stretched for the sake of convenience; God's love is perfect.

In a sense, divine love defies description. There is no neat little definition that encompasses all the avenues love may take. And because love cannot be packaged or bottled, many people today are pursuing a myth rather than seeking the love described in the Bible.

First John 4:7-8 helps us understand the true nature of love: "Beloved, let us love one another, for love is of God; and every one that loveth is born of God, and knoweth God. He that loveth not knoweth not God, for God is love."

John tells us at least two things—"love is of God" and "God is love." Norman Grubb wrote, "Love is exclusively a person."

John continues, "In this was manifested the love of God toward us, because that God sent His only begotten Son into the world, that we might live through Him. Herein is love, not that we loved God, but that He loved us, and sent His Son to be the propitiation for our sins" (vv. 9-10). The sacrifice of Jesus on the cross is a demonstration and also a definition of love.

What does this have to do with you and me? The Scriptures refer to believers as vessels (2 Cor. 4:7). A vessel is a container; God has made us to be His vessels, and He expects us to contain Him. A vessel is useless if it remains empty. But it is worse than useless if it contains the wrong thing. A basket that is full of apples cannot simultaneously be filled with oranges. Our lives can never contain Christ and His love until they are emptied of all that would rival for His place.

If our primary purpose in life is to contain Christ, to be filled with His love, then we would be wise to get on with the supreme business for which we were created.

What is love? How can we define it? Love is being filled with God. It is reflecting Jesus Christ in everything. That is why we are encouraged again and again to love as Christ loved.

Love Is Discerning

William Shakespeare wrote, "Love is blind, and lovers cannot see the pretty follies [petty faults] that themselves commit" (*The Merchant of Venice* 2. 6. 36).

Earthly love may be afflicted with a kind of blindness, but divine love is knowledgeable. The church at Philippi was strong and mature. They were a caring fellowship with few spiritual problems. In spite of their spiritual health, however, Paul prayed that they would abound in knowledgeable love: "And this I pray, that your love may abound yet more and more in knowledge and in all judgment; that ye may approve things that are excellent; that ye may be sincere and without offense till the day of Christ" (Phil. 1:9-10).

Paul's prayer suggests two facts about divine love: (1) It is knowledgeable, not ignorant; (2) It is discerning, not gullible.

Divine love has its eyes wide open. It knows the score. It is not stupid or excessively sentimental. And the result of this knowledge and discernment is the ability to approve what is best so that we may live pure and blameless lives.

My awakening to the life-changing power of God's love began during a serious illness while I was a student at Chicago's Moody Bible Institute. The school doctor recommended immediate surgery for the removal of a tumor. Because the tumor appeared to be malignant, the operation was followed by thirty X-ray treatments. I shall always remember the honest, loving concern of Dr. Titus Johnson, as he carefully explained that my condition could be fatal, and if not, the possibilities of my fathering children were remote.

During those trying days, a former Sunday School teacher sent me a booklet by James McConkey on the theme of God's love. As I read it, I began to see my need to love God supremely and to let His love operate through me. My sickness, the quietness of the hospital, the booklet about God's love, and the possibility of death were all blended by the Great Physician to awaken my consciousness to the supreme importance of God's love. Through it all, I caught a vision of the love of God and the exciting possibility of reflecting Jesus Christ to my world.

My hospital bed was, in a very real sense, my altar of sacrifice. I reminded the Lord of my deep desire to serve Him. I told Him that I wanted His will more than anything in life. I prayed, "Dear Lord, this hospital bed is my altar of sacrifice. If it pleases You, I'd like to be a *living* sacrifice. With Your enablement, I now yield myself to You to become a channel of Your love to reach others."

In the years since those crisis days, I have enjoyed good health, a strong body, and the unexpected gift of four sons. Shortly before his death Dr. Johnson wrote me, reminding me that God had graciously worked a miracle.

He was right, but the real miracle was that God had imbedded in me a sense of His love—love that is discerning, tender yet tough, fair and firm, with the ability to distinguish the true from the false.

Three Words for Love

The Greek language has three words for three different dimensions of love. The first word is *eros,* a self-gratifying love. *Eros* is a physical expression of love and passion-seeking satisfaction. Though it is gratifying, it is self-centered and short-lived.

Eros is not found in the Bible. It is used in pagan writings to describe the love between people of opposite sexes. C.S. Lewis says that *eros* is "that kind of love which lovers are 'in'" (*The Four Loves,* Harcourt Brace Jovanovich, Inc., p. 131). *Eros*—ask any schoolgirl—is strong, sweet, and sometimes terrifying! Yet, in spite of its intensity, it is a weak love. It needs divine help, without which it dies or becomes a demon.

The second Greek word is *phileo,* companionate love. This is the love that exists between good friends or between parents and children. It is characterized by affection, fondness, or liking. The name *Philadelphia* comes from this root word and means "city of brotherly love." Our word *philanthropy,* meaning "love of man," also has its source in *phileo.*

Dr. Kenneth S. Wuest described *phileo* as that love called out of one's heart by the pleasure one takes in the object loved (*Golden Nuggets from the Greek New Testament,* W.B. Eerdmans Publishing Co., p. 62). We feel this kind of love for people with whom we are familiar. We do not always know when affection begins; often we discover only after someone has gone just how fond we were of him.

By itself, *phileo* is a quiet, comfortable feeling for people we usually take for granted. Much of the solid, genuine happiness of our lives comes from our humble affections for each other. But *phileo* too needs divine help.

The third Greek word used for love is *agape,* an unselfish, sacrificial love. Wuest suggests that this is "a love springing from a sense of the preciousness of the object loved." It is a love of esteem, of valuing. The word carries the idea of prizing. It is "the noblest word in the Greek language" (*Golden Nuggets,* p. 63).

This word speaks of God's love for us and in us. The word is seldom found in classical Greek; the pagan world apparently was unaware of its reality. The source of *agape* love is God Himself.

God loves us because of all that He is, not because of what we are. *Agape* love seeks the good of others regardless of the cost. For God the Father, the cost was inexpressible. For God the Son, the cost was displayed at Bethlehem's manger and on Calvary's cross. *Agape* love does not merely care; it acts.

This is the love we desperately need in order to make sense out of the others. This is the love that brings substance and glory to *eros* and *phileo.*

W.E. Vine describes *agape* as "the chief characteristic word of Christianity." It is the foundation stone of any life in Christ. Without God's help, our other loves cannot even remain what they start out to be, or become what they promise. Only as God's love possesses us can any other love have a firm foundation.

Some time ago a woman told me that all her life she had been hungry for love. As a child, "Judy" would have done anything to win approval from her family and friends. She had always wanted her mother to hug her and her father to buy her gifts as tokens of their love.

Immediately after her graduation from high school, Judy

had married, but her relationship with her husband had never progressed beyond the physical level. She knew she still had not found any satisfying love, despite having four children. Nothing seemed to help the terrible emptiness inside.

Then one day a neighbor invited Judy to a Bible class in her home, where she heard the Good News that Jesus Christ loved her. Here was the love she had been looking for all her life; here was Someone who loved and accepted her just as she was. Eagerly she had invited Christ into her life and had begun at last to come alive.

Despite the joy of her newfound love, Judy remained saddened by the gulf between her husband and God. She seemed unable to convince him of Christ's love. Then one day her friend suggested that she should *demonstrate* the love of Christ to her husband, right in their own home. As she became concerned about showing love to her family, she began to realize how many things needed changing in her life. She had often nagged her husband and children; the Spirit of God taught her when to hold her tongue. Her housekeeping improved; her preparation of meals showed more care and originality; her excess weight disappeared. Instead of going back to bed after her husband left for work, Judy stayed up and enjoyed breakfast with the children, praying and reading the Bible with them before they left for school.

As God's love softened and changed her, Judy's love for her husband and children expressed itself in dozens of ways that softened her family too! One day her husband started out the door, then turned around and came back. He took her in his arms and kissed her good-bye—something he had not done in years! Later, as Judy tucked her five-year-old into bed, what a thrill it was to hear the child say, "Mommy, it's so nice at our home since we started loving Jesus, isn't it?"

Only through Jesus Christ filling us can our human love blossom forth in power and beauty.

Love Is the Greatest

3

"And yet show I unto you a more excellent way".

1 Cor. 12:31

What is the greatest quality in the world? The Bible says it is divine love!

A business firm commissioned an artist to design a new corporate logo. Two weeks later the artist submitted his design—attractive but quite simple—along with a bill for several thousand dollars. The client balked at the high price tag for such a simple drawing. "The high price," said the artist, "is for knowing what to leave out of the design."

In life, it is extremely important to know what to leave out.

In his booklet *The Tyranny of the Urgent,* Charles E. Hummel tells how he was brought up short by someone saying to him, "Your greatest danger is letting the urgent things crowd out the important" (InterVarsity Press, p. 4).

Attempting to be a channel of God's love never seems urgent, yet nothing is more important. In fact, seeking and demonstrating God's love is the highest pursuit as well as the greatest need of the church today.

We continually face the challenge in life to distinguish between what is good and what is best, between what is great and what is the greatest.

On my desk sits a sign bearing the pointed reminder: "Keep Off the Detours." Life is filled with interesting and attractive roads that, in spite of their allure, are *detours*. It is our responsibility to refuse anything that would deflect the magnetic needle of our calling. We must press forward toward what the Bible calls "the greatest of these"—love.

A More Excellent Way

To read 1 Corinthians 13 out of context is to miss its full impact, depth, and message. The Corinthians were a group of believers richly blessed with spiritual gifts from God. Apparently they had accented the spectacular gifts and minimized the less spectacular gifts. They were using their gifts as a source of pride.

Before exploring the nature of love, Paul reminded the Corinthians that spiritual gifts are given sovereignly by the Holy Spirit (1 Cor. 12:7-11, 28) for the building of the church, not for the building of self. These gifts are to be received rather than sought after.

However, Paul encouraged the Corinthian believers to "covet earnestly the best gifts" (1 Cor. 12:31). The word *covet* is the verb *desire*. Paul urged the congregation to eagerly desire the greater gifts—gifts that build up the entire church rather than those that are self-serving and self-building. Paul concluded that, as helpful as gifts may be, they are not enough. *What I am* is more important than *what I do*. The way of love does not replace gifts; love is greater.

After discussing spiritual gifts, Paul went on to say, "And yet show I unto you a more excellent way." Scholar Joseph A.

Beet renders this phrase, "a surpassingly *good* way I show you" (*A Commentary on St. Paul's Epistles to the Corinthians,* Thomas Whittaker, p. 228). J.J. Lias translates it, "I show you an eminently excellent way" (*The First Epistle to the Corinthians,* Cambridge University Press, p. 127). The Apostle Paul was simply saying, "Love is the greatest!"

The problem we face is that of selecting priorities. We must choose the best; we must go after the greatest good. We must always remember that love is the greatest.

Paul was not the only one to regard divine love as supreme. Peter came to the same conclusion. He taught the early church many things, but he rated love as the most important. "Above all," wrote Peter, "keep fervent in your love for one another, because love covers a multitude of sins" (1 Peter 4:8, NASB).

Notice that Peter placed love above *all* things. He called for fervent love among believers. We may fail in various areas of life, but let us make sure we do not fail to experience and reflect God's love, because, says Peter, "love covers a multitude of sins."

I have a Christian friend who, like most of us, has some glaring faults. Seldom is he on time. Often he is careless in following through with details. But as irritating and objectionable as his faults are, he abounds in fervent love for God and others. The abundance of love in his life goes a long way in covering his deficiencies. Love covers. Both Paul and Peter claim that God's love is the greatest.

Jesus' Call to Love

When we think of the great love chapter of the Bible, we immediately think of 1 Corinthians 13. But John 13 is also a great love chapter. Jesus said, "A new commandment I give unto you, That ye love one another; as I have loved you, that ye also love one another. By this shall all men know that ye are My disciples, if ye have love one to another" (John 13:34-35).

Later, Jesus repeated His commandment to "love one another":

This is My commandment, That ye love one another, as I have loved you. Greater love hath no man than this, that a man lay down his life for his friends. Ye are My friends, if ye do whatsoever I command you. Henceforth I call you not servants, for the servant knoweth not what his Lord doeth; but I have called you friends, for all things that I have heard of My Father I have made known unto you. Ye have not chosen Me, but I have chosen you, and ordained you, that ye should go and bring forth fruit, and that your fruit should remain; that whatsoever ye shall ask of the Father in My name, He may give it you. These things I command you, that ye love one another (John 15:12-17).

This command is echoed in Romans 13:8: "Owe no man any thing, but to love one another, for he that loveth another hath fulfilled the Law." When I love, I will not hurt another in any way. God's love in me fulfills the Law.

A New Commandment

Jesus presented three life-changing truths about love. The first was that to love is *a new commandment*.

The very mention of a new commandment brings to mind the old commandment. The Law was given to convince us of sin and our total lack before a holy God. The old commandment was our schoolmaster, bringing us to the place of faith in Jesus Christ (Gal. 3:24). "And they that are Christ's have crucified the flesh with the affections and lusts" (Gal. 5:24). The Law brings us to the place of recognizing and acknowledging our sinfulness (Rom. 3:20).

Some time ago, while waiting to board a plane at Chicago's O'Hare Airport, I became engaged in conversation with a businessman and his wife. After watching several jets shoot into the murky darkness, the woman remarked, "I wish I could vanish into space just like that plane and escape to start life all over again somewhere else."

She was a young and attractive woman, a woman of wealth and position; and yet her life was filled with emptiness and regret. Why did she want to vanish? Why did she want to escape? Because the ugly hand of the past was reaching into the present and spoiling her life. She wanted a new start.

Many people today would echo those words of dissatisfaction. Millions are seemingly driven by a similar haunting desire to begin all over.

Recently one of our national news magazines featured an article on Americans emigrating to South America and Australia. When interviewed, some of those modern "pilgrims" explained that they were naturally daring and were seeking excitement and adventure. Most of those going, however, expressed a desire for change. Distressed by the crime rate, social unrest, and the soaring cost of living, they wanted to "get away from it all." They wanted to start life over again somewhere else.

Have you ever wanted to get away from it all? Have you ever wondered what it would be like to have a new start in life?

Many people seem to think they can gain a new start by moving to a new area. Young people run away from home. Businessmen quit their jobs and seek new employment. Couples leave the community when one of the partners has been found to be unfaithful. But a new start is not necessarily found in a new place. It is not found in a new job or a new home. Only through God's forgiveness can you have a new start right where you are.

You must begin by acknowledging that you are sinful and in need of a Saviour. Have you ever acknowledged that Jesus Christ can meet your need? Have you, in faith, asked Christ to be your Saviour?

J.B. Phillips has translated 2 Corinthians 5:17, "If a man is in Christ he becomes a new person altogether—the past is finished and gone, everything has become fresh and new."

Once you have, in faith, received Jesus Christ and become a new person, you are to obey the new commandment of loving others.

A New Model

Often I am asked, "How can I communicate God's love in this dog-eat-dog world? Is it *possible* to demonstrate love?"

Jesus Christ modeled for us how to love. We are to love as He loved. He said, "Love one another, as I have loved you" (John 15:12).

How did Jesus love? In at least two ways Jesus modeled love for us:

1. By serving His disciples (John 13:3-5);
2. By sacrificing His life for the sins of the world (1 John 4:10).

Just before His death, Jesus, knowing who He was and why He had come into the world, took a towel and began to wash His disciples' feet. He showed that we are to communicate love by serving one another faithfully in the ordinary circumstances of life.

A pastor communicates love by being prepared in heart and mind to share God's Word with his people when they gather together for worship and ministry. Believers communicate love by listening, encouraging, and assisting each other. In a very real sense we can lay down our lives sacrificially for each other. Jesus is our model as we seek to be channels to a love-starved world.

A New Mark

"By this shall all men know that ye are My disciples, if ye have love one to another" (John 13:35). The world will not recognize that we are Christ's disciples by our elaborate programs, extravagant facilities, elegant music, or eloquent preaching. Our distinguishing mark is not a shepherd's staff or an ox's yoke. Nor is our mark the fish or fish hook. It is not even the cross or the crown. Our new mark is divine love. The three great apostles, Paul, Peter, and John, all agree that the way of love is the greatest of all.

Time magazine once gave a full page to the life of entrepreneur Aristotle Onassis, calling him "one of the last tycoons." When only 17 years old, Onassis left his family in Greece and traveled steerage to Argentina to make his fortune. He began with only $100, but by age 21 he was worth over $1 million. He gained a reputation as a ruthless, determined manipulator, and he lived for wealth and what it could buy. *Time* quoted Onassis, "All that really counts these days is money. It's the people with money that are the royalty now."

But life changed dramatically for Onassis when his son, Alexander, apparently the only person he cared for, was killed in a plane crash. "He aged overnight," observed a close associate. "He suddenly became an old man."

Frank Brady, in his book *Onassis,* concurs. "When his son died, so did he." Two years later, Onassis, afflicted by a neurological disorder, died with no one beside him except his daughter, Christina. In spite of his wealth, he was destitute of love.

In contrast, John and Elaine Beekman worked selflessly among the Chol Indians of southern Mexico for more than twenty-five years. In spite of John's ailing heart, and amid weariness and threats, they poured out their lives for the Chol. Three times John was at the brink of death, and three times his life was prolonged.

The Beekmans and their co-workers translated the New Testament into the Chol language and established a school for training church workers. The Chol church expanded to more than 13,000 members and became self-supporting.

John's heart finally gave out. As he was being taken to the hospital, he said weakly, but with a slight chuckle, to Elaine, "We've had a good life, darling, being channels of God's love."

Are we wasting our lives or investing them in love for others?

Paul's Lifetime Goal

4

"Though I speak with the tongues of men and of angels, and have not love, I am become as sounding brass, or a tinkling cymbal".
1 Cor. 13:1

I was moved by a newspaper article about a once lovely countess who had been caged like an animal for more than 40 years in a castle outside Milan, Italy.

She had been locked in a dingy room where she slept on rags on the floor, behind walls spattered with her blood.

Finally, at age 65, she was carried on a stretcher from her jail. No longer beautiful, she was an emaciated scarecrow. Her matted gray hair reached down to her thighs. She was nothing but skin and bones, with inch-long fingernails. She screeched in terror at the sight of her rescuers and babbled disjointed phrases in a dialect nobody understood.

How tragic are the results of being unloved!

I was also shaken by a small news item about a 14-year-old boy who took his own life because "no one seemed to care."

He had felt no love from anyone except his dog, and in a brief suicide note addressed to his parents, he left instructions for the dog's care.

"No one seemed to care." What a stark rebuke to the world's lack of love—or lack of sharing and showing it! It is quite likely that boy's parents really did care, but evidently they failed to show it, and his suicide illustrated sharply how minor deeds of lovelessness add up to major tragedies.

Gypsy Smith used to tell the story of one of his sons coming to his study on a day when he was very busy. To avoid being bothered, Gypsy offered the boy a special knife to play with, but the boy ignored it. He tried to interest his son in a number of other things but had no success. Finally he asked, "Son, what in the world do you want?"

The boy replied, "Daddy, I want you."

That is not a revolutionary statement of new insight; it is the sad experience of everyday life. When no one seems to care, the wild weeds of frustration, loneliness, indifference, emptiness, hostility, resentment, jealousy, and sometimes resultant criminal acts all grow to fill the holes gouged in peoples' hearts.

People of all ages can sense real love. When we show God's love to others, we will be amazed at the eagerness of their response. God, who is love, is revealed through His people's love.

The Apostle Paul was a tried and proven, battle-scarred soldier of love. Writing to hurting people who lived in a mixed-up culture, he wrote about lawsuits, strained relations, broken homes, discord, and immorality. He tackled tough problems head-on and provided practical guidelines for daily living. The love described in 1 Corinthians 13 is a down-to-earth, flesh-and-blood confrontation with life as it is.

The first three verses present our deep need for God's love. Paul compared the gift of love with the gifts of speech, prophecy, faith, benevolence, and martyrdom, and demonstrated beyond any doubt that God's love is greater!

Love Is Greater than Eloquence

"Though I speak with the tongues of men and of angels, and have not [love], I am become as sounding brass, or a tinkling cymbal" (1 Cor. 13:1).

The Corinthians prized the gift of speech. They enjoyed standing in the council and listening to the eloquence of their orators. Demosthenes, Sophocles, Euripides, and other silver-tongued speakers were the idols of the day.

The power of persuasive speech *is* a great gift, and throughout history powerful eloquence has stirred people to heroic deeds and bloody battles. Bernard of Clairvaux spoke, and thousands followed him to the Crusades. Patrick Henry declared his determination to achieve liberty, and a nation arose to fight for freedom.

Never will I forget Winston Churchill's eloquent speech of June 4, 1940 at Dunkirk:

> We shall fight on the beaches;
> we shall fight on the landing grounds;
> we shall fight in the fields and in the streets;
> we shall fight in the hills;
> we shall never surrender!

At other times, Churchill could lighten tense moments with humor or sarcasm. It is reported that Lady Astor, who disliked Churchill intensely, said, "Winston, if you were my husband, I'd put arsenic in your tea."

Without a moment's hesitation, Churchill replied, "Madam, if you were my wife, I'd drink it."

Without a doubt, human words have power. Words can win or wound, kiss or kill, inspire or infuriate. Paul reminds us that our words, minus the love of God, are like the tuneless crash of cymbals or the hollow sound of a brass gong, without orchestration or melody.

As the Lord listens to us, what does He hear? Is it the pure sound of love undefiled, or the blaring of brass and tinkling of cymbals? It would be better that some sermons were never preached and some anthems never sung than that love should be missing. Jesus said, "If ye love Me, keep My commandments" (John 14:15). He did not tell us to multiply our prayers and praises; He simply commanded us to love one another. Love is greater than words!

Christianity exploded in the Roman Empire when Christians reflected the love of Jesus. They proclaimed the Gospel through a practical demonstration of love for people. The first believers learned from Jesus Himself. Through His personal association with the despised and downtrodden, and His concern for the poor and afflicted, He showed them how to love.

Missionary David Livingstone could not always communicate the Gospel verbally to the people to whom he ministered, but those people always felt his love. Love has the agility to leap over language barriers to reach people. Love communicates.

A friend of mine who works with inner-city youth tells the story of a teenager from a New York ghetto who spent a week with him at a Christian camp. During the first few days of the camping period, he had become a Christian, having been won by the love of the work crew.

When the boy returned to the city, someone asked what it was that had moved him to accept Christ. He replied, "The way people cared about me. Everybody seemed interested in what was happening to me. Nobody ever loved me like that before."

People will respond to our words when they are woven in love! This young man had heard the Gospel, but he had never really seen God's love in action until those days in camp.

Gina came from one of the thousands of broken homes in the city of Chicago. She started drinking when she was just 12 years old. She quickly moved on to glue sniffing, and before long she was shooting heroin into her veins.

Sermons were boring to Gina, but when the people in one of the local churches began paying attention to her as a person, God's love began to reach her. She could not get over the fact that these people actually wanted her in their church. Only after she had received their love was she ready to listen and to understand the words that explained God's love for her in Jesus Christ. People are tired of words without love.

Love Is Greater than Prophecy
"And though I have the gift of prophecy . . . and have not [love], I am nothing" (1 Cor. 13:2).

Not only is love greater than eloquence; love is greater than prophecy!

What a gift prophecy is! The prophets not only spoke forth God's truth, but also, in many instances, foretold future events. Paul insists, however, that as desirable as prophecy is, this gift minus God's love equals zero.

Throughout the world people delve into astrology, hoping to get a glimpse of the future. Nearly 1500 newspapers in the United States print daily horoscope columns. Famous seers and so-called prophets have an enormous following of readers trying to gain some insight into tomorrow. For many people, determining the future is an obsession.

Paul realized the significance of the gift of prophecy, but he concluded that the prophetic gift without God's love is useless. It cannot compete with the dynamic love of God working in and through the lives of men and women.

D.L. Moody recounted that not until hearing Henry Moorhouse preach on John 3:16 for a solid week did he understand the power of God's love. Richard Ellsworth Day, in his biography of Moody, *Bush Aglow,* records Moody's own account of what happened to him at those meetings:

I never knew up to that time that God loved us so much. This heart of mine began to thaw out; I could not keep back the tears. I just drank it in. . . . I tell you there is one thing that draws above everything else in the world and that is love (Judson Press, p. 145).

After this happened, Moody, who was already a successful Christian worker, saw for the first time the secret of a winsome church:

The churches would soon be filled if outsiders could find that people in them loved them when they came. This . . . draws sinners! We must win them to us first, then we can win them to Christ. We must get the people to love us, and then turn them over to Christ (Day, *Bush Aglow,* p. 146).

Matthew paints a picture of those who will call, "Lord, Lord, have we not prophesied in Thy name?" (7:22) The answer is, "I never knew you: depart from Me, ye that work iniquity" (v. 23).

Love Is Greater than Insight

"And though I . . . understand all mysteries . . . and have not love, I am nothing" (1 Cor. 13:21).

Paul compares love with understanding "all mysteries," divinely inspired insight into hidden truths. In my travels I have met spiritual giants who have challenged me to greater living. I have occasionally been disappointed, however, to find that some believers are more concerned about hidden mysteries than about hidden people. They will chase a Greek word all through the New Testament but appear indifferent to the unconverted in their own neighborhoods or apartment buildings. Skill in unraveling the mysteries of God is desirable, but without love for others, it amounts to nothing.

It is one thing to know that love is the greatest gift; it is quite another thing to practice it. D.L. Moody described the result of his study of God's love:

I took up that word 'Love,' and I do not know how many weeks I spent studying the passages in which it occurs, *till at last I could not help loving people* [italics added]. I had been feeding on Love so long that I was anxious to do everybody good I came in contact with.

I got full of it. It ran out my fingers. *You* take up the subject of love *in the Bible!* You will get so full of it that all you have got to do is to open your lips, and a flood of the Love of God flows out (Day, *Bush Aglow,* p. 146).

Love Is Greater than Knowledge

"And though I have . . . all knowledge . . . and have not [love], I am nothing" (1 Cor. 13:2).

If knowledge were the golden key that could unlock the door to solving all human conflicts, our problems would be over. Man possesses more knowledge today than every before. Scientific learning progresses so rapidly that even the most brilliant cannot keep pace. But the sad truth is that these strides in knowledge have done very little to solve man's problems. In fact, in many ways, knowledge by itself compounds our problems rather than solving them.

Knowledge is a rare gem which we dare not handle carelessly. Yet there is nothing so hard, dead, and cold as knowledge without love. Knowledge by itself, said the apostle, is nothing.

D.L. Moody was frustrated before he experienced the power of God's love in his life. His congregations showed signs of falling away. He found himself wondering if the Gospel might need something added to it to make it attractive to people. While reading on a train from California, after attending a Sunday School convention, he recalled Henry Moorhouse saying to him four years earlier, "You are sailing on the wrong tack. If you will change your course, and learn to preach God's words instead of your own, He will make you a great power" (Day, *Bush Aglow*, p. 130).

Moody realized then that he had been desperately trying to explain what the Bible teaches before filling his soul with what it says. After Moorhouse left Chicago, Moody had not followed what he had learned from him. Instead he had taken a course in reading, and when he selected a text and started to preach, he would immediately depart from it. Now, sitting on the train, he recalled with new understanding what an old gentleman in Boston had told him years before: Young man, when you speak again, honor the Holy Spirit" (Day, *Bush Aglow*, p. 131).

That summer Moody made the rewarding commitment to give even his ignorance to Christ, and new life flooded his church. Even the August heat did not keep the people away. Moody realized humbly that his sermons now had divine power—power that had never been there in the parade of his own knowledge.

At the close of his ministry, Moody's advice to his successor was, "Dr. Erdman, give the people the importance of love. If they are right here, they will be right 95 percent of the time."

Love puts us in touch with God and the times. Love transforms doctrine into power. Love adds feet to facts and it results in action. The need of our day, as much as of Moody's day, is love to empower our knowledge.

A woman once came to me after a Sunday morning service and confessed, "I have been a Christian for 20 years now. During that time I have read many books on winning others, yet I do not know of anyone that I have led to the Lord. I have memorized Scripture and know how to meet the objections of the unconverted, but still I have brought no one to a decision. Why have I been so useless?"

My answer surprised her. "You are a fruitless Christian," I told her, "because your eyes are dry."

"I don't understand," she said.

So I explained, "You have failed not for want of knowledge but for lack of love for people. When you really love someone, you will care enough to lay down your life for them. Psalm 126:6 promises, 'He that goeth forth and weepeth, bearing precious seed, shall doubtless come again with rejoicing, bringing his sheaves with him.'"

She returned home to read the Scriptures and pray. As she prayed, her heart was strangely warmed, and her unbelieving sister came vividly to her mind. She got up from her knees to go to her, and with genuine tears threw her arms around her sister and admitted in love, "More than anything in this world, I want you to be a Christian!" Together they came to the meeting that night, and when I invited those who wanted to know the Lord to come forward, the two of them walked up together. The woman's sister had been won by a genuine expression of love.

Knowledge is important, especially in our age, yet it must be immersed in love to be effective. Paul warns, "Knowledge puffeth up, but love edifieth" (1 Cor. 8:1). Beware of the dichotomy between knowledge and love. I have observed hundreds of students who, although they have accumulated considerable knowledge, have lacked love. We need to pray for knowledge that is caring. Our goal should be academic excellence immersed in the love of Christ.

Knowledge without love is dead! But knowledge with love is dynamic!

Some years ago I visited a railroad man who was called the toughest man in town. As I attempted to speak to him of God, he cursed the church, the Bible, and me. He threatened to throw me out bodily if I ever returned to his home. As I made my watchful retreat, I said quietly, "Mr. Baldwin, God loves you, and I love you, too."

I was not prepared for what happened. Almost instantly he

melted. He fell to his knees and wept uncontrollably as he emptied his heart of hatred and sin. It was God's love that overwhelmed him. That rough railroader was beautifully changed. Knowledge without love is powerless, but together they are life-changing.

Love Is Greater than Faith

"And though I have all faith, so that I could remove mountains, and have not [love], I am nothing" (1 Cor. 13:2).

The faith referred to here is the kind that gets things done. Faith is an important gift. In fact, without faith we cannot please God.

When Jesus' disciples were not able to cast a demon out of a man who had been brought to them, they questioned the Lord saying, "Why could not we cast him out?"

Jesus answered them saying, "Because of your unbelief: for verily I say unto you, If ye have faith as a grain of mustard seed, ye shall say unto this mountain, Remove hence to yonder place; and it shall remove; and nothing shall be impossible unto you" (Matt. 17:19-20).

Make no mistake, faith is important! It is the foundation on which love builds. Faith is the basis, even though love is the summit. An individual must come to Christ in faith before he can know anything of God's love.

But—faith without love is nothing.

A group of New England pastors who met in Boston for three days to study love made a breakthrough that ignited their faith. One of the men who attended said, "We listened, learned, and loved. We were reconciled and brought together! The world will never really believe in the power of Christ until it can see us one in love and appreciation, respecting each other as persons, attempting to discover ever more clearly the power of the risen Christ."

Without the love of Christ nourishing us, we bring the powerlessness of a dead faith to a dying world. Paul prayed for the Ephesians, "That Christ may dwell in your hearts by faith; that ye, being rooted and grounded in love, may be able to comprehend with all saints what is the breadth, and length, and depth, and height; And to know the love of Christ, which passeth knowledge, that ye might be filled with all the fullness of God" (3:17-19).

Paul was so emphatically the apostle of faith that his conclusion about love is all the more convincing.

Faith is great, but love is greater.

Faith has priority, but love has preeminence.

Faith is the beginning; but love is the goal.

Faith connects the soul with God, and God is love.

Faith is the means that God uses to bring us into His love, but faith without love leaves us bankrupt.

Love Is Greater than Benevolence

"And though I bestow all my goods to feed the poor, and though I give my body to be burned, and have not [love] it profiteth me nothing" (1 Cor. 13:3).

All of us have given to help the poor—a dinner to the hungry, a donation to the underprivileged, a dollar to the crippled man as he holds out his tin cup. Prosperity imposes obligation. To have should mean to owe. The needy are all about us, but often benevolence is no more than a way to relieve a guilty conscience. It is too easy to write a check and dismiss our responsibility for caring. The emperors of Rome gave lavishly on special holidays to keep the masses under their control. They gave bread for empty stomachs and the circus for entertainment. But they gave without loving.

How humiliating it might be if others were to know the motives for our giving! Too often we give to others because of a feeling of obligation rather than out of a sense of gratitude for what God has given us. Psychologists are finding that many people, in spite of their prosperity, harbor guilt that stems from accumulation of material possessions. Some give because of this guilt. Others give to gain recognition. A man may make a donation to a cause because he desires another's praise. Like the self-righteous men Jesus condemned, he gives so that all can see (Matt. 6:1-2).

The life of the early church demonstrated a much different pattern of giving. Those first Christians had learned from Christ that it was impossible to belong to each other and still be indifferent to the needs of other members. The phrase used in Acts, "in common" (2:44, NASB), indicates their belief that God's gifts were meant to supply the needs of all and should be shared with others. What was not essential for their own needs they shared with the poor, and in doing so, they gave of themselves as well. As Bernard F. Meyer says, "We cannot but think that Jesus often invited the poor to eat with Him, rather than giving them a backdoor handout."

The church must return to this kind of caring. I know of churches that have formed "care units" to meet the physical needs of the poor with the ultimate purpose of meeting their spiritual needs.

This quality of giving can spring only from God's love. It is neither going through the motions to satisfy a requirement, nor a way to excuse ourselves from personal involvement. The love that is already present within us because of God's presence there bears fruit when we share our resources gladly. Unless we are motivated by God's love, we will be like the Pharisees who sounded the trumpets so everyone would notice that they were giving. The Bible says, "They have their reward" (Matt. 6:2). It is not so much what we give, but how we give it. It has often been said, "We can give without loving, but we cannot love without giving."

Love Is Greater than Martyrdom
"And though I give my body to be burned, and have not [love], it profiteth me nothing" (1 Cor. 13:3).

Martyrdom is farther from our experience today than it was at the time Paul was writing to the Corinthians. There were Christians in Paul's day who suffered the flames and the lions' teeth and endured other physical violence because of their deep love for Christ. Paul suggests, however, that martyrdom could result from something other than consecration. It could be motivated by fanatical devotion to a cause rather than love for Christ. Martyrdom may be more out of principle than out of love.

The war in Vietnam produced some spectacular instances of martyrdom. One young man set fire to himself in Washington, burning to death in order to publicly protest the war he felt was wrong.

The Buddhist monks who became fiery pillars to a pacifistic principle are modern-day martyrs for a cause.

Charles L. Allen, in his book *The Miracle of Love* (Revell, 1979), suggests that perhaps Paul had yet another thought in mind when he spoke of giving his body to be burned:

> This was a day when slavery was commonly practiced. Just as ranchers brand cattle today, human beings were branded as slaves in that day. The hot iron was applied to their flesh and those men wore that stigma for the balance of their lives. 'Though I give my body to become a branded slave. . . .' This is sacrifice in its most complete form. Yet—even such sacrifice is profitless without love.

A generation ago the plea for young people to love Christ enough to die for Him was common. Today the plea more often assumes that it takes as much courage to live for Him. To live in relationship to those around us is no easy calling. It calls for every ounce of commitment we can muster. Living the love of God is the greatest challenge, the highest calling to which a human being can respond. Someone has said, "Love is appealing, but its practice is appallingly difficult."

What Motivates You?

We humans are crafty creatures who rationalize so much that it is difficult to decide what our real motives are. Will you try an experiment? Stop reading for a moment. Look over your life. Analyze your failures, your restless spirit, your dissatisfaction. You will probably discover that love is the missing ingredient.

Part of the good news of the Gospel lies in Christ's promise to make us different when we come to Him. We need to heed the advice of Scripture, "Seek ye first the kingdom of God, and His righteousness; and all these things shall be added unto you" (Matt. 6:33).

John Calvin, commenting on 1 Corinthians 13:1-2, concluded, "For where love is wanting, the beauty of all virtue is mere tinsel, is empty sound, is not worth a straw, nay more, is offensive and disgusting."

The lifelong goal for many people is possessions. For others, abilities. Paul contrasts the gift of love with the gifts of eloquence, prophecy, knowledge, faith, benevolence, and even martrydom, and he concludes that any or all of these gifts are nothing when devoid of God's love.

Let me summarize this chapter with a potent equation: Life − Love = 0! Colossians 3:14 could well be translated, "Most of all, let love guide your life." This is a goal worth living for.

The Spirit of Love
5

"[Love] suffereth long, and is kind; [love] envieth not; [love] vaunteth not itself, is not puffed up".

1 Cor. 13:4

Our world is very much in a hurry. That's why we have instant tea, instant coffee, instant rice, and an *instant results mentality*. Three words seem to characterize our generation—hurry, worry, and bury. We certainly hurry and worry, only to ultimately bury.

A homemaker complained to her doctor, "I'm all run down."

To which he replied, "No, ma'am, you're all wound up."

Have you ever noticed that evil is often done in a hurry? On that night of our Lord's betrayal, He spoke to Judas and said, "That thou doest, do quickly" (John 13:27). On the mount of temptation, Satan offered Jesus "the kingdoms of the world" (Luke 4:5) and promised them *immediately* if Jesus would fall down and worship him. Satan promised Jesus a shortcut. Essentially he was saying, "You don't have to die on the cross to gain the kingdoms of the world. I'll give them to you in a hurry."

In contrast to an impatient world, God's love is supremely patient and kind.

As an artist blends colors to produce a painting, so Paul the apostle draws together the characteristics of love, which give us a portrait of Jesus. We could rightly say, "Jesus suffered long and was kind. Jesus never envied. Jesus vaunted not Himself." Every characteristic of love listed by Paul was true of Jesus.

As beautiful as that sounds, however, there is a catch: 1 Corinthians 13 was written not to describe Jesus but to describe what *we* are to be like. The questions are: Are *we* patient and kind? Are *we* free of envy and self-importance?

Love Is Patient

"[Love] suffereth long, and is kind" (1 Cor. 13:4).

The Greek word for the phrase "suffereth long" literally means "to have a long temper" as opposed to a short temper. It describes someone who takes a long time to become angry.

Exodus 16 describes the Children of Israel as they wandered through the wilderness. "And the whole congregation of the Children of Israel murmured against Moses and Aaron in the wilderness" (v. 2). The Lord could have responded by raining down fire, but instead, "Then said the Lord unto Moses, Behold, I will rain bread from heaven for you" (v. 4). God is patient.

Jesus Christ spent His life caring for others. Throughout His ministry, He went about healing the sick, feeding the hungry, comforting the bereaved—always helping others! And though He was often misunderstood, misused, and rejected, Jesus remained patient; He never stopped showing love.

The Saviour was long-suffering with His weak-willed disciples, who disappointed Him so often. He was merciful to the despised and the mentally disturbed. He was long-suffering with Pilate, with the Roman centurion, and with the crucified thief (Luke 23). Jesus suffered long and was kind even in His dying hours. After the nails had done their cruel work, He cried out, saying, "Father, forgive them; for they know not what they do" (Luke 23:34).

The story is told of two mountain goats who approached one another on a narrow ledge. Realizing that there was no room to pass, they reared and bucked, but neither budged. They backed up, charged, and locked horns again, but each held his ground. Again they parted and charged; then like Rocks of Gibraltar they stood unmovable. Finally the more sensible one knelt down and let the other climb over him. Both went merrily on their way. Sometimes we too must let people walk over us. Love is long-suffering.

Dr. Harry Ironside used to tell of a young man who, impatient because a church business meeting was not going his way, disrupted the meeting by shouting, "I want my rights! I want my rights!"

An elderly church member responded, "Did I hear our young friend say he wanted his rights? If he received his rights, he would be judged and sent to hell. Jesus Christ went to the cross to die for his 'wrongs' and make him right."

With that, the younger man apologized for acting out of impatience rather than love, and the meeting continued. Christian love is willing to suffer a long time.

Love Is Kind

"And is kind" (1 Cor. 13:4).

Goethe wrote, "Kindness is the golden chain by which society is bound together."

Our world is starving for kindness, the expression of a warm, sympathetic nature. Wordsworth described it as "the best portion of a good man's life." The word *kindness* comes from the same root as *kindred* and implies affection for those who are our own flesh and blood. Paul reminds us that kindness is a mark of Christian love; love acts kindly.

Kindness is also God's attitude toward us. In spite of our unloveliness, He keeps on being kind.

How can we show kindness when we have differences with those around us? We must keep four words foundational in our relationship with Jesus Christ as well as with others: "I'm sorry; I'm wrong."

At a management retreat, I urged Moody Bible Institute employees to be quick to use those words when the occasion warranted them. Many have discovered what a difference this spirit makes in their day-to-day relationships.

The world says, "Win through intimidation; take care of yourself first," but Scripture reminds us, "[Love] suffereth long and is *kind*" (1 Cor. 13:4).

Divine love is kind even when misunderstood. Love knows how to take heartache victoriously. The Greek verb translated "is kind" implies *active service*. In ourselves, we are often hasty, hotheaded, and unkind. God's love is not unkind; it actively seeks to show kindness.

Some years ago, I was misunderstood and criticized by people from whom I had expected support. I desperately wanted to retaliate, or at least argue for my side of the conflict. With bulldog determination, I clenched my fist, bit my lip, and managed to keep my mouth closed. But I was *not* kind.

A large part of being kind is being patiently willing to put up with abuse that comes our way. Usually that patience is needed most just when it is exhausted. Our tolerance wears thin, and our spirits of kindness melt.

I heard Vance Havner say, "A bulldog can beat a skunk any day—but it just isn't worth it." We need to take our grievances to the Lord instead of taking them out on others. Paul reminds us, "'Vengeance is mine; I will repay,' saith the Lord" (Rom. 12:19).

The kind of love described in 1 Corinthians 13 goes beyond our understanding, yet this is the kind of love God wants to communicate through us. It is constant in the face of neglect, ignorance, lack of appreciation, and even undeserved violence. When Stephen, one of the early church deacons, was being stoned to death, he prayed, "Lord, lay not this sin to their charge" (Acts 7:60). This kind of love is possible only through Jesus Christ. He gives us the capacity to love.

Someone has penned these words, which could be taken as a description of Christian kindness:

> Able to suffer without complaining;
> To be misunderstood without explaining;
>
> Able to give without receiving,
> To be ignored without grieving:
>
> Able to ask without commanding,
> To love despite misunderstanding;
>
> Able to turn to the Lord for guarding;
> Able to wait for His own rewarding.

A love that suffers long and is kind is beyond our natural ability. It is only as we experience God's love flowing through us that we can demonstrate that kind of love.

How much long-suffering and kindness do you have for others? How willing are you to put another person's desires above your own? Are you willing to go an extra mile, to turn the other cheek? Do you go out of your way to be cooperative and to show love through acts of kindness?

A pastor in Pennsylvania discovered two women living near

his church who seemed lonely and in need of help. Their reputation for behaving oddly and keeping to themselves made
them less than approachable.

The pastor asked one of the women in his congregation to
visit these women. She was courageous and kind but still was
fearful as she walked up the path to the run-down house.
When she knocked at the door, one of the women opened the
door and snapped, "What do you want?"

Assuring the women that she wanted only to be of help, the
visitor was allowed to come in and was led to a bedroom
where the woman's invalid mother lay, frowning and suspicious.

As the mother began to question her, the visitor remem-
bered all the neighborhood stories she had heard about these
women. She became frightened and wondered why she had
ever agreed to make the visit. But as they talked, she began
thinking about the love that Christ expressed to women just
like these two. "God loves these women," she thought, "and I
love them too!" What a change she sensed in herself as she
began to really listen and show compassion! Before leaving the
house, she put her arms around the big, straggly haired invalid
woman and gave her a hug and a kiss. Tears came to the elderly woman's eyes as her frown melted into a warm smile.
The kindness of Christ was nourishing someone starved for
love!

That single act opened the way for kindness to be multiplied
by many others in the church. Two families donated coal to
heat the house; another gave a refrigerator; many contributed
clothes. Someone arranged much needed medical care for the
elderly mother. Children sent cards and baked cookies. A man
began to take care of the women's lawn. A neighbor offered
the use of her telephone whenever needed. Another woman
took time to drive the daughter to the market for groceries.

Eventually, the new friendships led to times of prayer and

Bible study. Before long, both women received Jesus Christ as their personal Lord and Saviour. And it all started because they had been shown the love of Jesus Christ through kindness.

When the visits to this home first began, the women had often asked, "Why do you care? Why do you come?" What an evidence of the indwelling presence of Jesus Christ we present when we express to others the warm, loving kindness that is characteristic of our Saviour.

Love Is Not Envious

"[Love] envieth not" (1 Cor. 13:4).

"Envy," says a Latin proverb, "is the enemy of honor." Someone has defined envy as the sorrow of fools. Solomon described it as "the rottenness of the bones" (Prov. 14:30). William Shakespeare spoke of envy as "the green sickness." Envy, in contrast to love, destroys relationships.

Paul states that Christian love is never envious of anyone or anything. It is not possessive. Envy and jealousy are deadly in anyone's life. Cain's envy led him to murder his brother (Gen. 4). Envy caused Joseph's brothers to sell him into slavery. They were resentful because he was the favored son of Jacob (Gen. 37). The elder brother in Jesus' story of the prodigal son was envious when he heard the rejoicing over his wayward brother. Scripture says, "He was angry, and would not go in" (Luke 15:28). Both brothers missed the father's love—the younger because he had been rebellious, and the elder because he was envious.

Envy is resentment of the good fortunes of others. Envy says, "If I cannot eat, then I want all others to starve. If I cannot see in one eye, I want you to be blind in both eyes." Envy is hatred without a cure. It cripples us and prevents us from living victoriously.

Almost everyone has been envious at one time or another. If

allowed to grow, envy is a disease that disturbs the mind and causes physical illness.

"Wrath is cruel, and anger is outrageous," wrote Solomon, "but who is able to stand before envy?" (Prov. 27:4) Envy is relentless in its pursuit of the human heart. Envy observes no holidays; it works against love continually.

Envy is usually found in the carnal or unregenerate person. According to James, envy is a characteristic of earthly wisdom that results in confusion, disorder, and all kinds of evil: "But if ye have bitter envying and strife in your hearts, glory not, and lie not against the truth. This wisdom descendeth not from above, but is earthly, sensual, devilish. For where envying and strife is, there is confusion and every evil work" (James 3:14-16). The terrible results of envy were displayed in King Saul, who envied David so intensely that he lost control of himself and tried to kill David (1 Sam. 18).

In contrast, love rejoices when others excel. Jonathan, Saul's son, could have been smitten with the same disease as his father; but he dethroned envy with love. "He loved him [David] as he loved his own soul" (1 Sam. 20:17).

Because Jonathan overcame envy, the two men were able to form a friendship that brought blessing back to Jonathan. In those days it was the custom for the new king to search out the descendants of the former monarch and exterminate them. But David, on ascending the throne, asked, "Is there yet any that is left of the house of Saul, that I may show him kindness for Jonathan's sake?" (2 Sam. 9:1) He discovered that Jonathan had a son named Mephibosheth, who was lame in both feet. That son was royally treated because of David's love for Jonathan (2 Sam. 9:7, 13).

Love Is Not Proud
"[Love] vaunteth not itself, is not puffed up" (1 Cor. 13:4).

Falling in love is exciting. Most of us know that strong

sweep of emotion that leads us to forget ourselves and promise our beloved anything. We meet someone who helps us leap over the walls of our own self-centeredness. We stop being concerned about ourselves and start thinking only of our loved one. Without expecting it or working toward it, we spontaneously fulfill the law of God—at least toward one person—by loving someone else as much as we do ourselves! We have no desire or temptation to "puff" ourselves; our only concern is to build up the beloved. We take pride in his or her company, attention, and abilities. We are radiant, and everyone recognizes love in our behavior.

We discover, however, after a month or a year, that this lofty condition is temporary or at best, intermittent. Our old self-centeredness, which we thought we had set aside, reappears, demanding attention and recognition. Only as our human love bows before the love of God and allows His humility into that relationship can it become dependable and lasting.

Divine love does not seek the applause of the crowd but places itself below all others. God keeps His best gifts on the lower shelves. Humility precedes honor, but "an haughty spirit [goes] before a fall" (Prov. 16:18). The Apostle Paul said, "Knowledge puffeth up, but [love] edifieth" (1 Cor. 8:1). A "puff" is any sudden, short blast of wind; it does nobody any good. The love of Christ is not sudden or brief; it is eternal. Love edifies—builds up—forever.

A missionary was translating the word *pride* into a native language. To properly convey the meaning she wrote, "The ears are too far apart." Pride is simply an inflated head.

The proud have exaggerated ideas of their own importance. Their primary interests are in self. One of Aesop's fables tells of a fly who sat on the axle of a chariot and exclaimed, "What a dust do I raise!" Living near a superhighway, I have noticed that empty trucks make the most noise.

Our world says, "If you've got it, flaunt it. If you've got it, you know it. If you've got it, show it."

The Bible says, "Love does not brag."

A.W. Tozer said, "Humility is as scarce as an albino robin." And believe me, they are scarce!

"Nothing sets a person so much out of the devil's reach as humility," said the great preacher Jonathan Edwards.

Pride is one of the Christian's greatest enemies. It is often at the bottom of our biggest blunders. A young Scottish minister once stepped into the pulpit with pride and complete self-confidence, but the sermon he delivered affected his congregation like a double dose of sleeping pills. The message was a failure, and he knew it. As he left the pulpit in defeat, an elderly woman whispered, "Son, if you had gone up the way you came down, you would have come down the way you went up!"

A proud and puffed-up spirit shows that a person does not have a proper self-image. When we see ourselves as God sees us, we cannot help but be humbled.

When a committee from Jerusalem asked John the Baptist if he was the Messiah, he answered simply, "I am not."

"Then, who are you?" they asked.

John said, "I am the voice" (John 1:19-23). He plainly told them that he was not the way but just the messenger to show the way. John was so filled with love for Jesus that self-conscious pride was impossible. "He must increase," said John, "but I must decrease" (John 3:30).

Love is not bigheaded; it is bighearted. The greater a person's ability, the less boasting he needs to do. But the less ability one has, the more noise he is likely to make about it. Divine love allows us to see ourselves as we really are in the sight of God and to reach out humbly to others.

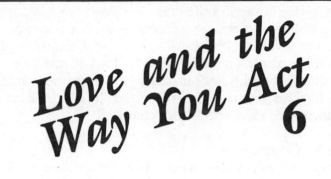

Love and the Way You Act

6

"[Love] doth not behave itself unseemly, seeketh not her own, is not easily provoked, thinketh no evil".

1 Cor. 13:5

Frederick the Great is reported to have said, "The better I come to know people, the more I love my dog."

C.W. Vanderbergh, in the same vein, wrote:

> To love the whole world
> For me is no chore:
> My only real problem's
> My neighbor next door.

These men may be displaying an honesty we sometimes lack. We do not often think of ourselves as unloving. In our sophistication we tend to think of our conduct as highly polished and considerate. We observe the important rules of etiquette, congratulate our friends on their accomplishments, and are usually able to put on quite a show of concern for our neighbors. We invite new neighbors in for coffee or give

Thanksgiving baskets to the poor. We may even smile at people we dislike or exchange greetings with our enemies.

But the love that Paul talks about in 1 Corinthians 13 is much more demanding. According to Paul, divine love never behaves rudely and is not self-seeking. It is not easily irritated and is not critical or suspicious of others. It is genuine concern for others, not mere social correctness.

Love Is Courteous

"[Love] doth not behave itself unseemly" (1 Cor. 13:5).

We know it is polite for a man to stand when a woman enters the room. We remember to say thank you for a gift. We know that a gentleman removes his hat on entering a house and that well-behaved children hop up to offer their seats to adults coming into a room. But many of these things we do merely out of a feeling of social responsibility. Sometimes they become a chore or duty, and we find little or no joy in doing them.

What a difference it makes when we truly love someone! How we jump to do little things that show our loving concern! When we love someone, we put that person uppermost in our thoughts and actions.

Politeness has been defined as "love in trifles." To do little things for others in a way that is genuine is to prove one's love.

Love does not behave in a discourteous manner. But greed does. Selfishness does. Fear does.

Watch yourself next time you are delayed in a traffic jam; do you lean on the horn? What's wrong inside of you when you try to crowd in front of another grocery shopper at the checkout counter? Real love is courteous and does not push other people around. Love expresses itself by making the way easier for someone else.

The one who allows the love of Christ to control him is not hard or harsh, crude or rude, rough or tough. He is courteous.

The word *courteous* orginally came from "court" and suggested the manners that prevailed in the palaces of kings and queens. Eventually it came to mean consideration for others in general.

Paul suggests this rule of courtesy: "Let nothing be done through strife or vainglory; but in lowliness of mind let each esteem others better than themselves" (Phil. 2:3). Charles B. Williams translates this verse, "Stop acting from motives of selfish strife or petty ambition, but in humility practice treating one another as your superiors."

We live in a world where everyone likes to be first. From the first time we grab the blocks away from our playmates, we think we must shove a little here and pull a little there and somehow come out on top. One-upmanship is the game of the day. "Get ahead," the world says. "Step on anybody you like as you climb to the top." Whether we seek the presidency of the PTA or the manager's spot in our department, we scheme to make ourselves look better than the person next to us. We tell ourselves that if we do not push ourselves forward and use others as stepping stones, we may be scoffed at as spineless victims of inferiority complexes who just cannot make the grade.

How different is God's approach! Paul described Jesus as One who was willing to make Himself of no reputation, One who humbled Himself until He became obedient even to death (Phil. 2:7-8). Jesus Christ is the supreme example of selfless love. The one who carries this attitude into his relationships will have no problem showing genuine courtesy to others.

Courtesy springs from love as the flowers spring from fertile soil. Regardless of background, a Christian man will become a gentleman and a Christian woman, a lady. Why? Because when God's love is planted in us, we grow to be like Christ. Love transforms us!

Love Is Modest

"[Love] seeketh not her own" (1 Cor. 13:5).

All of us battle daily with "superself," the desire to put ourselves first. Divine love does not seek the center stage. In fact, in God's program of things, we kneel before we rise. The way up is the way down. The secret lies in surrendering our will to the will of God, so that His way becomes our way.

Andrew Murray asked, "Do you want to enter what people call 'the higher life'? Then go a step lower down."

Joseph, of the Old Testament, literally went down into a pit, down into slavery, down into a dungeon for thirteen years. But because he humbly and faithfully did his work well, he was lifted up, and he eventually became the ruler of all Egypt, second only to Pharaoh.

Similarly, we must go down before we go up; we must go deeper before we go farther. Love walks softly and seeks not her own way. The greatest happiness in life comes from giving, not from getting. "Bear ye one another's burdens, and so fulfill the law of Christ" (Gal. 6:2).

A husband who had entered into a new relationship with Christ wanted to share it with his wife. Years before, he had decided that one chore he would never do around the house was carry out the garbage. He would do anything else gladly, but not that. Now, as he asked the Lord how he could get through to his wife, he could not seem to get around that garbage sack sitting by the back door. Finally, he stooped down, picked up the bag, and carried it out to the alley. His love for both God and his wife had grown past the point of wanting to prove anything. He was free to become a garbage carrier in love.

The Bible indicates that one of the signs of the end times is selfishness. "This know also, that in the last days perilous times shall come. For men shall be lovers of their own selves, covetous, boasters, proud, blasphemers, disobedient to parents, unthankful, unholy" (2 Tim. 3:1-2).

The ego-driven person thinks of himself as supreme and of others as unimportant. But if God's love is in us, we will not think that way. God's love is different. It is not a circle with self at the center but more like outstretched arms that reach people wherever they are and lift them up.

Love Is Not Irritable

"[Love] is not easily provoked" (1 Cor. 13:5).

Irritability is a product of our nervous, fast-paced age. We rush here and there. We don't know where we're going, but we're already ten minutes late! I am amused when I see shoppers in a department store become upset when they miss one section of a revolving door.

The center of irritability is self. But when we are practicing God's selfless love, we will be slow to become irritable.

Nowhere will the genuineness of our love be tested more than at home. Spirituality is not measured by our worship on Sunday morning but by our response when our son kicks his pajamas under the bed instead of putting them in the hamper, or when coats are hung on a chair instead of in the closet. The validity of faith is not discovered at the Lord's table on Sunday but at the breakfast table on Monday. But how often we entertain the stranger with smiles while our loved ones are hurt by our impatience. The toughest place to demonstrate love is at home.

An unknown writer warned, "Irritation in the heart of a believer is always an invitation to the devil to stand by."

Paul says that love "is not provoked." The word "easily," inserted before "provoked" in the *King James Version,* is often seized as an excuse for letting off steam, but this word is not found in any of the original manuscripts. Perhaps some of the translators in 1611 thought Paul was going a bit too far, so they added the word *easily!*

A boy went riding one day with his father, who drove with little regard for anyone. He fussed and fumed, bellowed and shouted at the other drivers as he drove through town. Finally they arrived home.

Later that day, the boy went out in the car with his mother. As they drove peacefully along, the boy asked, "Mom, where are all the idiots?"

"Idiots?" asked his mother, puzzled.

"Yes. This morning when I was out with Daddy, we saw seven of them!"

The sin of irritability has spoiled the peace of many homes. Some people are harder to get along with than a bale of barbed wire. Love is the only antidote for irritability.

Legend has it that Jonathan Edwards, third president of Princeton and one of America's great preachers, had a daughter with an uncontrollable temper. As often happens, this fault was not known to many people outside the family.

A young man fell in love with this daughter and asked to marry her.

"You can't have her," was the abrupt answer of Jonathan Edwards.

"But I love her," the young man replied.

"You can't have her," repeated Edwards.

"But she loves me," replied the young man.

Again Edwards said, "You can't have her."

"Why?" asked the young man.

"Because she is not worthy of you."

"But," he asked, "she is a Christian, isn't she?"

"Yes, she is a Christian. But the grace of God can live with some people with whom no one else could ever live!"

The secret of a good temper is more than self-control; it is Christ-control. All of us have dynamite in the cellar, and whenever we try to get along without God and the power of His love, we must expect explosions.

A student said to me, "I lose my temper, but it's all over in a minute."

I answered, "And so is the hydrogen bomb. But think of the damage it produces!"

A bad temper is something you never lose by trying to lose it. When you lose control of yourself, you lose the ability to think and act as a rational human being. You become, in a sense, subhuman.

"A wholesome tongue is a tree of life; but perverseness therein is a breach in the spirit" (Prov. 15:4). Paul instructed Timothy, "The servant of the Lord must not strive, but be gentle unto all men, apt to teach, patient, in meekness instructing those that oppose [him]" (2 Tim. 2:24-25).

Henry Drummond spoke about temper in his address on love, "The Greatest Thing in the World":

It is the intermittent fever which bespeaks unintermittent disease within; the occasional bubble escaping to the surface which betrays some rottenness underneath; a sample of the most hidden products of the soul dropped involuntarily when off one's guard; in a word, the lightning form of a hundred hideous and unchristian sins. For a want of patience, a want of kindness, a want of generosity, a want of courtesy, a want of unselfishness, are all instantaneously symbolized in one flash of Temper.

Hence it is not enough to deal with the Temper. We must go to the source, and change the inmost nature. . . . Souls are made sweet not by taking the acid fluids out, but by putting something in—a great Love, a new Spirit, the Spirit of Christ. . . . This only can eradicate what is wrong, work a chemical change, renovate . . . the inner man (Hodder & Stoughton, pp. 38–39).

But what if we have been offended? How can we confront our brother in love and refrain from acting irritably? Here are some suggestions:

1. Begin by affirming your appreciation or affection. If confronting a family member, earnestly assure him, "I love you very much."

2. Speak softly. Communication decreases as volume increases.

3. Avoid such sweeping indictments as, "You are never on time!" Instead, refer specifically to the incident that has displeased you.

4. Use the correct approach, showing a willingness to understand the other. Someone has said, "If you want to gather honey, don't kick over the beehive."

5. Conclude your conversation by reaffirming your appreciation or affection, whether you have achieved your purpose or not.

Divine love is sensitive to others; it does not respond to others out of irritation.

Love Does Not Think Evil

"[Love] thinketh no evil" (1 Cor. 13:5).

Love is optimistic; it looks at people in the best light. Love thinks constructively and senses the grand possibilities in other people.

What a delightful atmosphere in which to live! How warming and invigorating to step into the brightness of this kind of love, even for a few minutes.

Everyone longs to feel important, to do something special, to be assured of his worth. Young people in particular often struggle with a poor self-image. Their problems with a negative self-image contribute to the fact that suicide ranks high among the causes of adolescent death.

God calls us to be expressions of His love to the people of our world. If we can communicate His love to others, affirming them rather than expecting the worst, we will truly be lights to brighten dark lives.

Dr. George W. Crane, author and social psychologist, has written a pamphlet called "The Compliment Club (The Hopkins Syndicate). To qualify for membership in this club, one must pay three sincere compliments a day, one to each of three different persons, for a month. The aspiring member is encouraged to compliment even complete strangers.

Crane's belief is that love cannot replace dislike or indifference at a moment's notice; it requires development of a definite technique and skill in approaching people. Love grows through showing appreciation and dies without it. "You can sincerely compliment your worst enemy, for no human being is totally lacking in merits," says Crane.

He tells stories of how compliments have changed people's lives. A woman working in a millinery house thought that Laura, who worked across the room from her, was snobbish and aloof. One day, however, to fill her quota of compliments, she said, "Laura, do you know that every time I glance up I see your head silhouetted against the window? I think you have the prettiest profile and hair of anyone I know."

Laura looked up startled, and then began to cry. "That's the first kind word anybody has said to me in all the seventeen years I have worked here," she said. All that time she had been hiding her loneliness behind pseudosophistication.

"Friendship," says Crane, "is a flower. To obtain a lovely flower, somebody must do the work of planting the seed, watering and cultivating it."

Isn't that what Jesus did? When He stopped to ask for water from the Samaritan woman (John 4:7) and when He told Zaccheus He was going home to dinner with him (Luke 19:5), He was giving compliments, showing He believed these people were worthwhile. He did the same when He ate with the despised publicans and sinners, and when He accepted the invitation of the Pharisees.

What an important way to show Christian love—to look for

the good in people and help them recognize it, to let them know that you believe good of them rather than evil. We Christians ought to be skilled social detectives, ferreting out the good points in all our associates.

Thinking no evil applies not only to our relationships but also to ourselves. Love casts out the evil thinking that spoils our daydreams and our quiet moments. Thoughts are the seeds of future deeds. Believers who would never do evil sometimes visit evil places in their thinking. You become what you think. "It is the thought of man . . . by which man works all things whatsoever. All that he does and brings to pass is the vesture of a thought," said Thomas Carlyle.

A young man emerging from an evil place unexpectedly met his pastor on the street. "I'm sorry," said the young man, "I had no business being there."

The wise pastor jolted the young man by saying, "When you came out and I saw you, you lost only your reputation. When you went in, and only God saw you, you lost your character."

Thousands of people have good reputations but no character. Omniscient God knows us completely.

Paul begs Christians to bring "into captivity every thought to the obedience of Christ" (2 Cor. 10:5). God cannot only cleanse the soul and heal the body; He can also cleanse the mind as He pours in His love.

A university student once approached me after a lecture and said, "I'm a Christian, but I'm up and down. My life is not constant." I suggested going to his room to further discuss his needs. His reluctance was so obvious that I began to feel that my visit to his room would reveal his problem.

He finally consented, and we went to his room. I scanned the room with its pictures and magazines, and quickly knew his trouble. Though upright in his conduct, the young man was filling his mind from pulp magazines and suggestive pictures. No wonder his experience was up and down! I counseled with him and I am happy to report that he was able to change his thought life and find stability. After graduating from the university, he went on to seminary and today has his own pastorate.

The Scriptures fill our minds with hope. The love of Christ flows into the hungry places of our souls and nourishes us. Grenville Kleiser gives us this advice:

> Watch your thoughts, keep them strong;
> High resolve thinks no wrong.
> Watch your thoughts, keep them clear;
> Perfect love casts out fear.
> Watch your thoughts, keep them right;
> Faith and wisdom give you light.
> Watch your thoughts, keep them true;
> Look to God, He'll govern you.

When my gasoline tank registers empty, I know it is full—that is, it is full of air. But the automobile was not built to run on air. To displace the air, I must fill it with gasoline.

God's cure for evil thinking is to fill our minds with that which is good. "Finally, brethren, whatsoever things are true, whatsoever things are honest, whatsoever things are just, whatsoever things are pure, whatsoever things are lovely, whatsoever things are of good report; if there be any virtue, and if there be any praise, think on these things" (Phil. 4:8).

The phrase "think on these things" suggests that we take an inventory. Love notices and concentrates on honesty, justice, purity, loveliness, and goodness—but not on evil.

That kind of thinking is possible only through the power of the indwelling Holy Spirit. He loves spontaneously. With Him inside us, we begin to love as Christ loved, seeing people as He sees them. But He does not work unless we allow Him to love through our thoughts and our actions.

Start with the first person you meet today. Is it your wife?

Your husband? The elevator operator? The bus driver? The paper boy? Maybe you are not in the habit of giving any greeting beyond an unintelligible grunt. Look at that person in a new way: here is someone God's love can touch through you. See what comment you can make, what question you can phrase, that will make him feel good. Let him know someone really cares.

On the other hand, if you don't really care, you can just go on using the old recipe for an unloving life:

Think about yourself.

Talk about yourself.

Use *I* as often as possible.

Mirror yourself continually in the opinion of others.

Listen greedily to what people say about you.

Expect to be appreciated.

Be suspicious.

Be jealous and envious.

Be sensitive to slights.

Never forgive a criticism.

Trust nobody but yourself.

Insist on consideration and respect.

Demand agreement with your own views on everything.

Sulk if people are not grateful to you for your favors.

Insist on being repaid for services you render.

Be on the lookout for benefits to yourself.

Shirk your duties if you can.

Do as little as possible for others.

Love yourself supremely.

Be selfish.

That recipe is guaranteed to make you miserable! Love, on the contrary, never acts in these ways. Peter writes, "Seeing ye have purified your souls in obeying the truth through the Spirit unto unfeigned love of the brethren, see that ye love one another with a pure heart fervently" (1 Peter 1:22).

Love
Tough and Tender
7

"[Love] rejoiceth not in iniquity, but rejoiceth in the truth".
1 Cor. 13:6

Some think of God's love as spineless. To the contrary, God's love is the strongest force in the universe. Divine love is tough even though it is tender. When truth suffers, love grieves, but when truth triumphs, love rejoices.

Love Abhors Evil

"Rejoiceth not in iniquity" (1 Cor. 13:6).

Divine love never rejoices in sin—my sin or the sins of others. Love cannot find satisfaction in wrong. When you read that delinquency is at an all-time high, what does it do to you? When you hear about four boys bludgeoning a man to death, what do you feel inside? When you read of an innocent girl attacked as she sleeps or of a child kidnaped and brutally slain for money, what is your reaction? When a thousand times a day, somewhere in this country, a gavel drops and a judge says, "Divorce granted!" does it bother you?

Love cannot rejoice in the evil of others. Some people like to sin vicariously, by reading gossip papers and pornographic literature. My love could be measured by what I enjoy reading and viewing. God's love finds no cause for joy in evil.

In addition to a secret love of sin, all of us have a contrary tendency to rejoice in the unloving characteristics of others. We enjoy seeing the mote in our brother's eye and ignoring the beam in our own! (Matt. 7:2-4) We seek to lift ourselves by putting others down. How deceitful we are!

Love, however, refuses to capitalize on the shortcomings of others. Love is caring—for better or for worse. Love is active concern for the growth of those we love. The essence of love is working for someone to help him develop.

To recognize another's sin and yet still work for his good shows strength, not weakness. It is true that Jesus went about doing good, but His goodness was firm and His words were strong. He called forth the best in the people He met but did not overlook their sin in order to "be nice." He occasionally offended even His disciples and relatives, for He was obedient to a higher loyalty. Though His was a mission of love, Jesus said, "Think not that I am come to send peace on earth: I came not to send peace, but a sword" (Matt. 10:34). Those who, in love, insist on righteousness must be prepared to stand against opposition. "The best way to show that a stick is crooked is not to argue about it or to spend time denouncing it, but to lay a straight stick along side it," said D.L. Moody.

Yes, Jesus was loving and kind, but when it came to evil, He was just. God's love never rejoices in the wrong but always in the right.

Love Enjoys the Truth

"[Love] rejoiceth in the truth" (1 Cor. 13:6).

The love Paul speaks of shows its strength in its concern for truth. When John Huss was about to be martyred, his tormentors called on him to give up his teachings. Huss answered, "What I have taught with these lips, I now seal with my blood."

Preacher Vance Havner observed, "Some Christians who once championed sound doctrine beat a retreat once in a while and from stratospheric heights announce that they will not 'stoop to controversy.' When a man contends for the faith in New Testament style, he does not stoop! . . . Contending for the faith is not easy. It is not pleasant business. It has many perils. It is a thankless job, and it is highly unpopular in this age of moral fogs and spiritual twilights. This is a day of diplomats, not prophets. It is nicer to be an appeaser than an opposer. It is the day of Erasmus, not Luther; of Gamaliel, not Paul."

God's truth is all-important and worthy of our life and of our death. It is significant that in the early church, doctrine preceded fellowship. "And they continued steadfastly in the apostles' doctrine and fellowship" (Acts 2:42). Truth is vital. "The wisdom that is from above is first pure, then peaceable" (James 3:17). Each of us seeks peace, but it cannot be at the expense of truth. Purity precedes peace as doctrine precedes fellowship.

In the year 1939, the Spanish Civil War was almost over. Just outside Madrid, the rebel General Mola prepared to attack. Someone asked which of his four columns would be the first to enter the beseiged city. To the inquirer's surprise, he replied, "The fifth." General Mola was simply saying that his most important forces were the band of rebel sympathizers already in the city, already fighting for him behind the loyalist lines.

General Mola's remark coined the term "fifth column," a synonym for traitorous forces. During World War II, it was a fifth column in Norway that brought about that country's collapse. Norway's leader, Vidkun Quisling, became a puppet premier of Adolf Hitler's German Nazis, and when, at the end of the war, Norway was freed, Quisling was put to death for treason.

Betrayal is an ugly business and yet very common in history. Down through the centuries, even the church has had its Quislings. Some, professing the Christian faith, have attacked the authority of the Scriptures, denied basic Bible doctrine, and sowed division, discouragement, and doubt. They have even challenged the foundational truth that salvation is by faith in Jesus Christ alone.

Opposition from within the church—*apostasy*—is clearly acknowledged in the Bible. People who once professed the faith, and still call themselves believers, become the enemies of the faith. They say to the church and to the world at large, "The things the Bible teaches aren't what they seem to be. This truth is not a truth. That fact is not a fact."

The Greek word from which we get the word apostasy means "a falling away, a rebellion or revolt." In New Testament times, to apostasize meant to desert a station or a post. The word was used by the Greek biographer Plutarch to describe a political revolution.

Apostasy has left its tragic wake in every generation. The church was still in swaddling clothes when Peter described how bad things would become. He warned of "false teachers" who would bring in "damnable heresies, even denying the Lord who bought them" (2 Peter 2:1). And it has been just that way. Apostasy has always been a deadly, all-out warfare. Apostasy discredits the Christian faith. The Bible tells us that apostasy will run its course and then disappear forever under God's eternal judgment.

What is the source of apostasy? It is the mind and heart of Satan as Jesus revealed in the Parable of the Tares (Matt. 13). He said the kingdom of heaven is like a farmer who sowed good seed in a field, but when the seed sprouted and grew, it came up among weeds.

The servants were greatly troubled. "Didn't you plant good seed?" they asked.

"Yes," he said. "My seed was good. But an enemy has sowed the weeds. Don't pull them now. Wait until the harvest. Then we'll gather the wheat and burn the weeds."

"The good seed are the children of the kingdom; but the tares are the children of the wicked one; the enemy that sowed them is the devil" (Matt. 13:38-39). Apostates are Satan's agents, his fifth column inside the church. The little New Testament Book of Jude tells us that they have "crept into the church" by deceit (v. 4).

What can you do to combat this evil? At least four things:

1. *Recognize evil.* Many Christians neither see nor hear with discrimination. An alarm in our minds and hearts should sound when we hear or read a message that says that the Bible is not the Word of God. We should catch the slightest whisper suggesting that there is a way to eternal life other than by Jesus Christ.

Almost always, false teaching will pretend to honor Christ; in fact, most apostate groups profess to "go by the Bible." We need to be like the Bereans, "who searched the Scriptures daily" to see whether the teaching they heard was correct (Acts 17:11).

2. *Resist evil teaching.* If you find an error, *do* something. Raise a firm yet gracious question. If error is there, warn others. Jude says we are to "contend for the faith . . . once delivered unto the saints" (v. 3). Only "the faith" shows the way of salvation. Anything less or more does not. You have a responsibility to see that the faith brought to you is handed on unaltered.

3. *Do not lend aid to evil.* The little Book of 2 John contains the burning warning, "If there come any unto you, and bring

not this doctrine [that is, the one Gospel], receive him not into your house, neither bid him God speed; for he that biddeth him God speed is partaker of his evil deeds" (vv. 10-11). How easily we can slip over to Satan's side!

4. *Finally, renew!* Especially, renew love. "Keep yourselves in the love of God," says Jude, as he closes warnings against apostasy (v. 21). Love abhors evil but rejoices in God's truth. How is your love for Jesus Christ? Anything that comes between you and your Lord, any controversy, any sin that is unconfessed, any coolness, may be the first step toward apostasy.

Keeping yourself in the love of God means walking close to Jesus Christ. It means day-by-day obedience. It means feeding on the Word of God. It means participating in the fellowship of the local church.

Someone has said the Christian life is like riding a bicycle: if you want to stay upright, you have to keep going.

So, walk on with the Lord—today, tomorrow, and every day. Abhor evil. Rejoice in the truth. Contend for the faith. Watch and pray and serve. And Christ will keep you in the way of life everlasting.

The Strategy of Love
8

"[Love] beareth all things, believeth all things, hopeth all things, endureth all things".

1 Cor. 13:7

Divine love seeks to forgive and restore wherever possible. That does not mean that we should be insensitive to sin. Known sin must be faced and adequately dealt with. But wherever there is doubt, love covers and leaves the judging to God.

Love Covers
"[Love] beareth all things" (1 Cor. 13:7).

The word "beareth" in 1 Corinthians 13:7 is the Greek word *stegō*, which literally means "to cover like a roof." Love is a retreat which shelters from the storms of life. *Love covers as a roof covers.*

A great aid in helping us accept the failures of others is remembering how God has covered our sins—sins of long ago

71

and sins of today; sins of the body, of the soul, and of the spirit; sins of omission and of commission. The psalmist says: "As far as the east is from the west, so far hath He removed our transgressions from us" (Ps. 103:12). The prophet declared, "Thou wilt cast all their sins into the depths of the sea" (Micah 7:19). The Lord says, "I have blotted out, like a thick cloud, thy transgressions" (Isa. 44:22). Isaiah affirmed, "Thou hast cast all my sins behind Thy back" (Isa. 38:17). God not only forgives but also forgets: "I will remember their sin no more" (Jer. 31:34). The Bible exhausts the possibility of language in telling us how completely God forgives. God's love covers us as a roof covers us, sheltering us from the storm of His wrath against sin.

What does this have to do with our love for others? "He who cannot forgive others breaks the bridge over which he must pass himself," wrote George Herbert.

When a brother fails, what do we do? Do we lift him up or cast him aside? Do we cover his faults or whisper about them? Do we engage in character assassination or try to work directly with the one in trouble? Unkind talk hinders the work of God a thousand times over. Critical tongues close church doors to hundreds of people. Unnecessary negativism breaks the hearts and health of many pastors. Someone has said, "A critical tongue is like Samson's foxes with firebrands on their tails going among the cornstalks of the Philistines."

When Andrew Jackson was being interviewed for church membership, the pastor said, "General, there is one more question which I must ask you. Can you forgive all your enemies?"

Andrew Jackson was silent as he recalled his stormy life of bitter fighting. Then he responded, "My political enemies I can freely forgive; but as for those who attacked me for serving my country and those who slandered my wife—Doctor, I cannot forgive them!"

The pastor made it clear to Jackson that before he could become a member of that church and partake of the broken bread and the cup, his hatred and bitterness must be confessed and dealt with before God.

Again there was an awkward silence. Then Jackson affirmed that if God would help him, he would forgive his enemies.

We may be called on not only to forgive our enemies but also to forgive our *friends* and *relatives*. When people very dear to us do not respond to us the way we would like, our anger toward them can tie us in knots and drain our effectiveness. Whether the friend or relative is actually at fault matters little. We can respond to him with quiet annoyance, a violent burst of temper, a crying spell, a sudden withdrawal, a jealous act, or an unkind remark. None of these is the response of love.

A minister I know tells how an experience of being forgiven changed his ministry. He had been too proud to have any of the members of his congregation considered more spiritual than he. Phyllis, one of the new members of his church, was so in love with Christ that she had an exhilarating influence on others in the congregation. The minister couldn't stand it! First, he became angry after he had asked her to give the story of her conversion as part of the Sunday evening service—not because of her story, but because several people commented that it had been the best service in months. *He* had been preaching regularly at those other services!

Then he began to encounter such comments as, "Phyllis thinks it would be a good idea," or "Phyllis suggested. . . ."

He found himself looking for ways to prove that his spirituality was superior and that she needed him. He looked for opportunities to show her that she really didn't know as much about spiritual things as she thought she did.

Phyllis, though just a new Christian, finally asked for a confrontation. She said, bearing the conflict in love, "You are my pastor, and I need you. We seem to be fighting each other. We shouldn't do that. We're on the same side." She even asked his forgiveness for causing him discomfort.

For two and one-half hours they talked. The pastor felt humbled, even embarrassed. But this new convert helped him find himself. He was forgiven in a genuine outreach of love, and he in turn could ask forgiveness as he confessed the competitive, jealous spirit that had obstructed his ministry.

What a release! Within a few months his whole congregation felt the new freedom. His sermons improved. Phyllis' spirit of love, which had borne his unjust combat, enabled him to let go of the bad feelings he had harbored.

Phyllis too, profited from being able to forgive rather than allowing bitterness to grow. "I will not permit any man to narrow and degrade my soul by making me hate him," wrote Booker T. Washington.

An unforgiving spirit blocks the forgiveness of God. A delicious sense of peace comes to the one who learns how to forgive. Love bears all that is placed on its shoulders and covers all that is placed beneath its wings.

When you are tempted to uncover another's sin, remember the Scripture: "Be ye kind one to another, tenderhearted, forgiving one another, even as God for Christ's sake hath forgiven you" (Eph. 4:32). What a measure of a forgiving spirit!

Some time ago a terrible forest fire devastated an area near where I was living. The effects of the fierce blaze were thoroughly depressing. As I walked through the charred forest, I doubted if anything had survived the inferno. All looked hopelessly dead; blackness prevailed. Six months later I returned again and discovered a miracle. A lush mantle of green had covered the darkness, filled in the wounds, and hidden the scars. I walked in the midst of nature's profusion of goodness and prayed, "Dear Lord, let Your love flow through me *to cover* the shortcomings and the scars of life that make all of us difficult to love. Give me a forgiving spirit. Amen."

Love covers as a roof.

Love also covers as a blanket. When Noah lay naked in a drunken stupor, his two sons Seth and Japheth entered his tent walking *backward* and *covered* him with a blanket (Gen. 9:23). They had no desire to disgrace their father.

The word *stegō* ("beareth"), in addition to describing a roof's covering, suggests the privacy and confidentiality of a blanket's covering. First Peter 4:8 reminds us, "Love covers a multitude of sins" (NASB). "Hatred stirreth up strifes, but love covereth all sins" (Prov. 10:12). "He that covereth a transgression seeketh love, but he that repeateth a matter separateth very friends" (Prov. 17:9).

Love also supports, as pillars support a roof. Are we supportive? Or would we sometimes like to see others fail? Love seeks, by word and deed, to support others.

Some years ago I decided to write or speak to a very special half-dozen friends who had greatly influenced my life. I wanted to be supportive.

While conducting services in Glasgow, Scotland, I had a thrilling opportunity to express my thanks and love to my Scottish grandparents for all they had meant in the life of my father. As I communicated my sincere love and support, they responded with tears of repentance to the message of salvation. Their spiritual awakening probably began because of loving support.

Later I wrote to a boyhood employer to express my appreciation for his deeds of kindness and his sterling character. In response, he too became receptive to the Gospel.

Divine love covers and protects and supports.

Love Believes

"[Love] . . . believeth all things" (1 Cor. 13:7).

Love takes the kindest view possible of people and circumstances. Love searches for what is good and gives the benefit of the doubt. Divine love is eager to believe the best and has faith in God.

Some years ago in Pittsburgh, a group of Christian businessmen saw very practical results of this expression of love— believing in people—as they began to show concern for some men who were unemployed. As they spent time with these unemployed men, they began to love them and to pray with them and for them.

During the next 19 months, 200 of the unemployed men found jobs. It became apparent that most of them were finding jobs on their own as this fellowship of love gave them increased confidence in themselves and renewed faith in God's personal concern for them. As a result of Christ's men believing in them, they were able to believe in themselves and move ahead.

One man said that after the first meeting with the Christian businessmen, he began to pray regularly that he would find a job. Some time later, while preparing for his daily time of prayer, he stopped and said to himself, "Mel, you've just been praying for work. Perhaps it's time to pray that the Lord will strengthen your faith."

The next day the phone rang, and a man who had interviewed him some weeks before asked if he was still looking for employment. The very next day he went to work.

Love has faith. Love trusts. Love believes in, inspires, lifts up.

The results of these men's prayers—new opportunities for employment, in contacts with people who were hiring—were not coincidences. The men who were communicating God's love through prayer had no magic formula. But the results they saw were far beyond their limited human means.

Similarly, Christians who minister in the inner city keep discovering what happens when people come in contact with love that expects the best of them. Some inner-city youth who have floundered through school with Ds, demerits, and detentions, not caring one bit about the marks they were making, have come alive when they have met Christ through the efforts of loving Christians. For the first time they have found a reason for trying, a purpose in doing their best. Many have turned their lives around and graduated from high school instead of dropping out. One fellow said, "Before I met the Lord I had a D average going into my senior year. The school told me, 'You can quit.' But when I heard how much Christ really loved me, I prayed, 'Christ, if You're real, You better do something in my life, 'cause I need it.' I came back to school and made the honor roll at the end of my senior year, passed my college boards, and they let me in college."

Divine love is not naive or gullible; it discerns between the true and the false. But having done so, it believes in what is good and trusts in God.

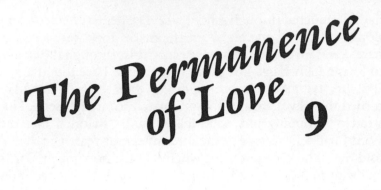

The Permanence of Love

9

"[Love] never faileth, but whether there be prophecies, they shall fail; whether there be tongues, they shall cease; whether there be knowledge, it shall vanish away".

1 Cor. 13:8

We live in a fascinating technological age. Man has split and fused the atom, placing tremendous energy at his disposal. He has attained speeds of travel unknown to any other generation.

In 1927 Charles Lindberg crossed the Atlantic, flying at a speed of about 100 miles an hour at an altitude of 5,000 feet. Today our jet aircraft fly more than 2,000 miles an hour at 80,000 feet. A supersonic trip between New York and Paris is now shorter than three hours. Serious study is being given to hypersonic transport at speeds up to 7,000 miles an hour. United Airlines estimates that by 1990 rockets will be sufficiently developed for commercial transportation, so that we will be able to blast off from Chicago and make a soft landing in Manila, 17,000 miles away, in about 45 minutes. Stupendous, isn't it?

We have seen more material changes in the last 100 years than in all recorded history. And yet, despite all our technological advancement, we still have not discovered how to live together in harmony. As Vance Havner observed,

We can fly like the bird,
And swim like the fish;
If we could only learn
To behave like men—we'd
Be doing something.

Lillian Smith, author and outspoken champion of racial equality, says the twentieth century is becoming the age of human relations. Suddenly we are only a few hours from everyone on earth, and we can share answers to temporal conflict.

At the same time, modern technology has given us new instruments and insights with which we can examine and understand ourselves. "It has crept upon us so quietly," she wrote in *The Journey,* "we have hardly noticed. But it is one of the significant events of the twentieth century: these groups of men and women, finding their tongues, sloughing off the old mutism and doing it just as science gives them the means of worldwide communication. Not arguing, not debating, not defending and entrenching their past mistakes. Not on trial. Simply saying, 'It was this way with me.'"

Too often we have not provided opportunity for people to express how it is with them. In many churches we can get together with 400 or 4,000 people on Sunday morning and yet not really know anyone. We can participate in a significant worship service without ever getting to know the person sitting with us in the pew.

A minister in the pastoral care department of one of Chicago's newest hospitals believes that the Christian church today has a tremendous potential which has not been tapped. "Our churches are worship-centered," says Larry Holst, "and project-centered, but not person-centered. . . . Christian fellowship is coming to see ourselves as we are—the splendor and the grandeur of man created in the image of God, as well as his misery; the potential of man in Christ, as well as his sinfulness. If we could get our congregations to be sensitive to the interpersonal feelings and relationships that are so crucial to people, I think we could turn many of our 'sleeping giants' into powerhouses of God's healing love."

What most often causes weakness in our churches is the absence of a demonstration of God's love to one another.

Jess Moody contends, "We will win the world when we realize that fellowship, not evangelism, must be our primary emphasis. When we demonstrate the Big Miracle of Love, it won't be necessary for us to go out—they will come in. . . .

"People don't go where the action is, they go where Love is" (*A Drink at Joel's Place,* Word Books, Inc., pp. 24, 36).

The infant church in the Book of Acts was a warmhearted, Spirit-filled, loving fellowship, and it was effective in reaching its world.

The ancient sophist used to say, "Nothing will last." To the contrary, Paul announces that divine love will last.

Earthly Things Fail

Yes, earthly things fail. The word "fail" in 1 Corinthians 13:8 is from the Greek *peptō,* "to fail." The original Greek presents two pictures. The first is of a bad actor being hissed off the stage. Of course, love is not like this; it lives on, even on the stage of eternity. Love is never hissed off the stage. The other picture is of a fading flower with falling petals. Love never withers, fades, nor falls away. Love never loses its place.

This is the same word used by Jesus in His Parable of the Foolish Man who built his house on the sand. When "the rain descended, and the floods came, and the winds blew . . . it fell [*peptō*] and great was the fall of it" (Matt. 7:27). In contrast,

the wise man built on the rock and his home did not fall
(*peptō*).

Divine love does not fall. It does not collapse. Earthly love
fails because we are temporal. Divine love lasts because it is
built on Jesus Christ, who is eternal and never fails.

Peter speaks forcefully of human frailty. "For all flesh is as
grass, and all the glory of man as the flower of grass. The grass
withereth, and the flower thereof falleth away [*ekpiptō*]: but
the Word of the Lord endureth forever. And this is the Word
which by the Gospel is preached unto you" (1 Peter 1:24-
25). The fading, perishing quality of man is contrasted to the
unfading Word of God. Earthly things fail.

When we wish to speak of lasting things, we often speak of
the everlasting hills and the unchanging heavens, but even
these symbols of permanency change. The Bible says, "All the
hills shall melt" (Amos 9:13). As for the unchanging heavens,
we read, "As a vesture shalt thou fold them up, and they shall
be changed" (Heb. 1:12). Let's remember, "The things which
are seen are temporal; but the things which are not seen are
eternal" (2 Cor. 4:18).

All about us we see the earth wasting under the powers of
corruption. Giant trees, once monarchs of the forest, are now
bent and broken with age. All nature groans under this death
process.

Where are the lavish, exotic hanging gardens of Babylon?
They are all gone. Where are the majestic temples of Greece?
For the most part, they are broken reminders of the Golden
Age. The great empires of yesterday have been led to the tomb
by the hand of time.

Death uproots and pulls down all creation. Every field has a
grave, every city a cemetery. This ugly invader not only turns
creation's beauty to ashes but also brings the creature to dust.
Death darkens the eyes of those we love; it eventually shakes
our own limbs and shuts the door on this life. Mortality reigns

in our bodies. Death starts at birth. Earthly things fail.

In contrast, love is eternal. Though everything else is mortal, love is immortal. When all else fails, love never fails.

Spiritual Gifts Fail

[Love] never faileth, but whether there be prophecies, they shall fail; whether there be tongues, they shall cease; whether there be knowledge, it shall vanish away" (1 Cor. 13:8).

I do not think Paul is underestimating the preeminence and permanence of God's love. Spiritual gifts are God's provision for a period of time, but divine love is for all time and even eternity.

Prophecy and knowledge will be set aside when their purposes are complete. Tongues shall cease or simply stop (*pauō*). All spiritual gifts are passing; they are temporal, not eternal.

Paul makes another point: spiritual gifts not only are passing but also are incomplete. "For we know in part, and we prophesy in part. But when that which is perfect is come, then that which is in part shall be done away" (1 Cor. 13:9-10).

Paul reminds us that spiritual gifts are "in part," that is, fragmentary. But one day all that is partial will be completed, and in that day love will reign supreme.

Jealousy over spiritual gifts had gripped the Corinthian Christians. This is probably why Paul stressed love as the greatest gift for each member of the body of Christ, no matter how unimportant he might seem. Love was for the Corinthians; love is for you too.

The history of the world has been one of greed, selfishness and war, rather than of love. Ralph Waldo Emerson, in *Man, the Reformer,* wrote, "Love would put a new face on this weary old world in which we dwell as pagans and enemies too long, and it would warm the heart to see how fast the vain diplomacy of statesmen, the impotence of armies, and navies, and lines of defense, would be superseded by this unarmed child. Love will creep where it cannot go, will accomplish that by imperceptible methods—being its own lever, fulcrum, and power—which force could never achieve."

Love is powerful beyond our imagination. Jesus Christ demonstrated the ultimate power of love in His life and in His death. The Cross is the great illustration of the conquering force of God's love.

Love Never Fails

Since Jesus is the personification of each characteristic listed in 1 Corinthians 13, it would be accurate to say that Jesus never fails.

In reality, everything in this life is fallible. "The world," wrote John, "passes away" (1 John 2:17). Business sometimes fails. Governments fail. Fame can fail. Friends often let us down. Health fails. Yes, everything fails except that which is centered in Christ: "Christ in you, the hope of glory" (Col. 1:27).

The disciples failed. When Jesus was arrested in Gethsemane, "all the disciples forsook Him, and fled" (Matt. 26:56). They let Him down.

The Apostle Peter failed. After Christ's arrest, Peter followed from afar and denied Him three times (Mark 14:54, 66-71). He had said he would die with Christ, yet he openly denied Him.

Thomas failed. When the disciples spoke of the Resurrection, he doubted and said, "Except I shall see in His hands the print of the nails, and thrust my hand into His side, I will not believe" (John 20:25).

When Jesus was on the cross, His mockers cried, "Come down" (Matt. 27:40). It would have been very human for Him to come down; but it was divine for Him to stay there.

The love that God gives to you and me never fails; it is trustworthy and faithful even when all else fails.

It is comforting to know that the disciples' failure did not alter Christ's love for them. His unfailing love allowed them to be restored. Peter wept bitterly at his denial (Matt. 26:75) and was later allowed to reaffirm his love (John 21:15-17). Thomas cried out, "My Lord and my God" (John 20:28). The disciples came back for cleansing and restoration.

We in the twentieth century fail Him too, but Jesus never fails, for He is God. His love is eternal. The most exciting adventure in life is to be controlled by God's love, for then all that we do will have eternal value. The command He has given us is: "These things I command you, that ye love one another" (John 15:17).

Millions of people viewed Michelangelo's famous Pieta when it was on exhibit at the New York World's Fair. The sculpture of the crucified Christ in the arms of Mary has been called marble in rhythm. Someday this masterpiece will crumble, and the name of its creator will be forgotten. But a deed done in love will last forever. To be motivated by God's love is to live with eternity's values in view. The great art of the masters will all pass into oblivion, but our acts of love will abide. Love never ends.

Recently I visited the 110-story, 1,454-foot Sears Tower, the tallest man-made structure on earth. It is a fantastic architectural feat, but someday its tons of concrete will be broken and its designer's name will be forgotten. And yet a cup of cold water, given in love, will break on the shores of eternity. In a world gone mad with greed and hate, how wonderful to know that love never dies! Love is never obsolete. Love never fails.

Let us pray daily for this gift of love. When we come to the close of this life, most of us will say, "We did not love enough."

May we experience the greatest marvel of all time, the greatest realization of ourselves; may we humbly seek the the openness to God's love that will enable our family and friends to feel loved by us and to say in wonder, "God is here!"

The Supremacy of Love

10

"And now abideth faith, hope, love, these three; but the greatest of these is love".

1 Cor. 13:13

Life at the longest is amazingly short. The Bible uses several metaphors to convey just how brief it is.

Job says, "My life is wind" (Job 7:7), and, "My days are swifter than a weaver's shuttle" (Job 7:6). Have you ever watched a weaver's shuttle? It moves so fast that you can't distinguish its movement. It's just a blur.

The psalmist compares life to a fading flower or a falling leaf: "As for man, his days are as grass; as a flower of the field, so he flourisheth. For the wind passeth over it, and it is gone" (Ps. 103:15-16).

The writer of Chronicles says, "Our days on the earth are as a shadow, and there is none abiding" (1 Chron. 29:15).

And Psalm 90:9 reminds, "We spend our years as a tale that is told."

James (4:14) asks, "What is your life? It is even a vapor, that appeareth for a little time, and then vanisheth away."

Life is so short that the wood of the cradle rubs up tight against the marble of the tomb. Added to the brevity of life is that fact that we had nothing to say about being born and yet we are here, and we *must decide* what we will do with this thing called "life." Only once can we live it. We dare not waste it. We must fulfill its potential to the best of our ability

Life for some is power; they want to rule others. For others, life is things or money or education. Some cry, "Fame!" Many cry, "Status," or "Success." What is your cry?

We have only one life to live. Let's make sure we choose the greatest good. Thousands come to the end of life only to discover that they have missed what was most important.

The Scriptures make it clear that one lifetime goal is supreme: *love!* This is the noblest pursuit in the whole world. Nothing else compares.

As the Apostle Paul concludes his treatise on love, he zeros in on the three great qualities of faith, hope, and love.

Faith

"And now abideth faith" (1 Cor. 13:13).

The Christian life begins with an act of faith. Paul writes, "For by grace are ye saved through faith; and that not of yourselves; it is the gift of God: not of works, lest any man should boast" (Eph. 2:8-9). We come to Jesus Christ in faith, believing. Each one acknowledges his need for the forgiveness of sin and sees in Christ God's provision for sin.

Edwin Arlington Robinson, in his poem, "Credo," writes,

I cannot find my way: there is no star
In all the shrouded heavens anywhere.

Left to ourselves, it is impossible to find our way. Jesus stated plainly, "I am the way . . . no man cometh unto the Father, but by Me" (John 14:6).

The Christian life not only begins with faith but continues in faith. The writer of Hebrews reminds us, "But without faith it is *impossible* to please Him" (11:6, *italics added*).

One can earn a living without faith in God. One can marry without faith. A house can be built without faith. Conceivably, one could become a millionaire without faith. But without faith, it is *impossible* to please God. The challenge is to grow in faith as we seek to please God.

Hope
"And now abideth . . . hope" (1 Cor. 13:13).

Dr. Victor Frankl, an Austrian psychiatrist who spent three years in a concentration camp, observed that a prisoner did not continue to live very long after hope was lost. But even the slightest ray of hope—the rumor of better food, a whisper about an escape—helped some of the camp inmates to continue living even under systematic horror (*Man's Search for Meaning*, Simon & Schuster).

The world we live in generally defines *hope* as "to wish" or "to desire very much." For example, we say, "I hope I'll get the job," or, "I hope I passed that exam."

In the Bible, the word *hope* is related to faith and trust. The root idea is to patiently wait for something. Job, for example, suffered incredible loss and intense pain, yet he responded, "Though He slay me, yet will I trust in Him" (Job 13:15).

Listen to the Apostle Paul: "For whatever was written in earlier times *was written for our instruction,* and through *perseverance* and the encouragement of the Scriptures we might have *hope*" (Rom. 15:4, NASB, *italics added*).

Romans 15:13 goes even further: "May the God of *hope* fill you with all joy and peace in believing, that you may abound in *hope* by the power of the Holy Spirit" (NASB). The Lord wants us to overflow with hope.

David wrote, "I *wait* for the Lord, my soul *does wait*, and *in His Word do I hope*" (Ps. 130:5, NASB, *italics added*).

The Bible is a *hope* book. Our God is the God of *hope*. One of the ministries of the Holy Spirit is to enable us to grow in hope. As we continually allow the Holy Spirit to live through us, He causes hope to abound.

I contend that the finest books are yet to be written. The best churches are still to be grown. The most comprehensive program of evangelism is yet to be conceived. The greatest medical discoveries are in the future. Biblical hope excites us, as it did missionary William Carey, "to attempt great things for God" and "to expect great things from God."

Love

"But the greatest of these is love" (1 Cor. 13:13, NASB).

Throughout the New Testament we are directed more than 55 times to love others. That tells us something about the supremacy of love. Following are just a few samples of the commands to love:

"Love your enemies, bless them that curse you, do good to them that hate you, and pray for them which despitefully use you, and persecute you" (Matt. 5:44).

"Jesus said unto him, Thou shalt love the Lord thy God with all thy heart, and with all thy soul, and with all thy mind. This is the first and great commandment. And the second is like unto it, Thou shalt love thy neighbor as thyself" (Matt. 22:37-39).

"A new commandment I give unto you, That ye love one another; as I have loved you, that ye also love one another. By this shall all men know that ye are My disciples, if ye have love one to another" (John 13:34-35).

"Let all your things be done with charity [love]" (1 Cor. 16:14).

"For, brethren, ye have been called unto liberty; only use not liberty for an occasion to the flesh, but *by love serve one another*. For all the law is fulfilled in one word, even in this: Thou shalt love thy neighbor as thyself" (Gal. 5:13-14, *italics added*).

"I therefore, the prisoner of the Lord, beseech you that ye walk worthy of the vocation wherewith ye are called, with all lowliness and meekness, with long-suffering, forbearing one another in love" (Eph. 4:1-2).

"Husbands, love your wives, even as Christ also loved the church, and gave Himself for it" (Eph. 5:25).

"Flee also youthful lusts, but follow righteousness, faith, charity [love], peace, with them that call on the Lord out of a pure heart" (2 Tim. 2:22).

Faith, hope, and love are three important lasting virtues; but of these three, love abides supreme because heaven is a world of love. In a very special way, heaven is the dwelling place of God and therefore a place where divine love stands supreme. God the Father, who so loved the world as to give His Son to die (John 3:16), is in heaven. God the Son, the Lamb of God, who so loved the world that He shed His blood for sinners, is there. God the Holy Spirit, who causes God's love to abound in us in this life, is there. Love reigns unrivaled.

Heaven has no pollution or defects. When we get there, we shall find everyone perfectly whole and lovely. The whole church, ransomed and purified, will be there and shall be presented to Christ as a perfect bride without spot or wrinkle (Eph. 5:27). Every believer will be full of love for God and for others. Love will be mutual, complete, and eternal. Love is without a doubt supreme.

For 55 years Amy Carmichael served Christ and the people of India. She was a channel of God's love, especially to the children. Often I have read this poem* of hers as a prayer:

> Mender of broken reeds,
>   O patient Lover,
> 'Tis love my brother needs,
>   Make *me* a lover.
> That this poor reed may be
>   Mended and tuned for Thee,
> O Lord, of even me,
>   *Make a true lover.*
>
> Kindler of smoking flax
>   O fervent Lover,
> Give what *Thy servant lacks,*
>   *Make me a lover.*
> That this poor flax may be
>   Quickened, aflame for Thee
> O Lord, of even me
>   *Make a true lover.*

---

*Frank Cottoughton, <u>Amy Carmichael of Donavhur,</u> Christian Literature Crusade, p. 224; *italics added.*)

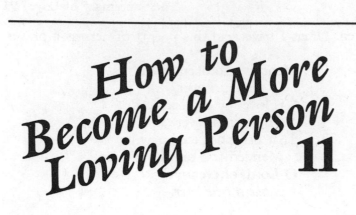

How to Become a More Loving Person 11

"Follow after [love]".

1 Cor. 14:1

Goals are important! All the activities of life—from the corporate board room to the baseball diamond—are oriented toward goals. The businessman's goal is to serve people and at the same time increase profits; the ball player wants to entertain people and reach home plate. All of us are motivated, to one degree or another, to achieve certain measurable goals.

The accomplishment of any goal requires at least two things: discipline and determination. Someone has given us this brief formula for reaching a goal:

Plan more work than you can do, then do it.

Bite off more than you can chew, then chew it.

Hitch your wagon to a star,

Hold your seat and there you are.

In chapter 2, I described my experience of choosing my lifetime goal to be a channel of God's love. This may be your goal too. But how can we become a more loving people? Let me suggest five steps toward becoming a channel of God's love.

Step One

The source of all love is God, for "God is love" (1 John 4:8). In order to love, we need to go back to the source of love. The very first step is to recognize Jesus Christ as our Saviour and Lord. He is God's gift of love to us. Without knowing Him, we will find true love impossible. Jesus said, "Except a man be born again, he cannot see the kingdom of God" (John 3:3).

We need to face the fact that in ourselves we are not whole; we are not well; we are not capable of making it alone. Sin is missing the mark of God's standard of holiness, and we all have done that. Sin is willful disobedience or lack of obedience to God's written Word and to the living Word, Jesus Christ. The Scriptures remind us, "All the world may become [is] guilty before God" (Rom. 3:19). Charles Spurgeon wrote, "One might better try to sail the Atlantic in a paper boat, than to get to heaven on good works."

When we understand that Christ's sacrifice is God's remedy for sin—that God in His love designed this whole magnificent way of salvation so that we could be complete as persons—our only reasonable response must be to ask His forgiveness for our sin. "But as many as received Him, to them gave He power to become the sons of God, even to them that believe on His name" (John 1:12). When we believe God and receive His answer to our dilemma, we become children of God! That's what He said—*children of God!*

To become a truly loving person, one must know God. Love is not a law or a code but a Person. This truth is one of the most remarkable things about the Christian faith. God knew we could not love until we had felt it, experienced it. So He expressed His love in human form—Jesus Christ—so that we human beings could grasp the patience, the kindness, the humbleness, the confidence, the optimism, and the joy that is contained in His perfect love.

Several former drug addicts are saying the same thing. On heroin from four to sixteen years, they came to Jesus Christ because they had tried everything else and had found no way out. John Giménez of New York City describes the group's experience of delivery from drugs through the Person of the Holy Spirit:

God brings His Holy Spirit into messed-up humans. That bursting forth of the Spirit within us is so peaceful and beautiful and sweet! We struggled so hard for so long to keep our bodies satisfied, and suddenly here was this wonderful Holy Spirit satisfying both our flesh and our spirit. . . . When we come home to God we get loved like we never have been loved before by anyone. We can walk with our heads up and smiles on our faces. . . .

Since we discovered that God really loves us, and it doesn't matter any more all the terrible things we have done, then we can try to help other people make the same discovery we made. . . . We know what it feels like to be lost. But we know now what it feels like to come home. We can see all the wonderful possibilities in a person. In a girls' prison, for instance, we can tell them, "God loves and cares for you." We can see ahead what God has for them when they come to Him. They can be fit mothers and loving wives. We know that God can do this for them because He has done so much for us.

The first step in becoming a more loving person is a personal saving relationship with Jesus Christ.

Step Two

We need to make God's love our lifetime goal. There is magic in having a goal.

This chapter began with attention focused on the Bible phrase, "Follow after [love]" (1 Cor. 14:1). The word "follow" connotes strenuous activity. It is the same word used to express Saul's relentless pursuit of the early Christians (Phil. 3:6). It is the word employed by Paul when he wrote, "I press toward the mark for the prize of the high calling of God in Christ Jesus" (Phil. 3:14). Paul is saying that we must make God's love our primary aim.

The gift of love is a prize to be won. It is the pinnacle of grace. By using the phrase, "Follow after," Paul seems to be urging us to be jealous of anything that would detract or hinder in our pursuit of this ideal. Consciously and subconsciously, each hour of the day and each day of the year, we must follow patiently and persistently after love. Let's make love our aim.

Step Three
We must earnestly pray for God's love. That's what Paul did: "And this I pray, that your love may abound yet more and more in knowledge and in all judgment; that ye may approve things that are excellent; that ye may be sincere and without offense till the Day of Christ" (Phil. 1:9-10).

The word "abound" comes from the Latin word meaning to overflow like the breaking waves of the sea. We would do well to begin each day asking the Lord to make this discerning love literally overflow in our lives.

Step Four
We must seek the fruit of the Spirit. Paul says, "The fruit of the Spirit is love" (Gal. 5:22). Let's not become worried by or impatient with God's timing. Fruit comes slowly. Remember that it takes a seed, a flower, pollination, warm sunshine, cold rains, and contrary winds to produce the finished fruit. That's true in life too. Our lives are made up of sunshine and rain,

blue skies and black, harsh winds and pruning shears. All of these work to produce this precious fruit called love.

In counseling young people in many parts of the world, I have observed that the primary goals they are seeking are love, joy, and peace. Isn't it interesting that the Bible tells us that "the fruit of the Spirit is love, joy, peace"? (Gal. 5:22) The goals of our young people can be realized when they allow the Holy Spirit to produce His fruit in their lives.

Are we yielding to the Holy Spirit? Do we know what it is to demonstrate love? All other gifts we may possess are less important than this particular fruit of the Holy Spirit. The fruit of the Spirit is the reproduction of the life and love of Jesus Christ in us.

In order to understand how to love, we must experience the power of God's love in our lives. Paul told the believers at Rome, "The love of God is shed abroad in our hearts by the Holy [Spirit who] is given unto us" (Rom. 5:5).

Many people make the mistake of struggling to produce the fruit of the Spirit without ever yielding themselves to the Holy Spirit Himself. This kind of effort is a waste of time. *The secret of the fullness of love is the fullness of the Holy Spirit.*

The Scriptures plainly teach that when we receive Jesus Christ as Saviour we actually become the dwelling place of the Holy Spirit. "Know ye not that ye are the temple of God, and that the Spirit of God dwelleth in you?" (1 Cor. 3:16) This is a staggering truth! Think of it—God the Holy Spirit living in us all the time!

In times past, God was in the tabernacle and then in the temple. That was where He displayed His glory. But where is He now? The Bible says, "Christ in you, the hope of glory" (Col. 1:27). The moment we receive Christ, the Holy Spirit comes to live in our bodies.

The word "dwell" in 1 Corinthians 3:16 has a beautiful depth of meaning: to settle down to stay, permanently, as we do in our own homes. The Holy Spirit is a personal, permanent guest. The Holy Spirit is God in us *all the time*.

But He is not there just to be taken for granted. The Holy Spirit may be grieved because of our carelessness. Paul warns, "Grieve not the Holy Spirit of God, whereby ye are sealed unto the day of redemption" (Eph. 4:30). The word "grieve" means to cause sorrow. G. Campbell Morgan asked, "How would you like to be compelled to live with somebody who was everlastingly grieving your heart by his conduct?" How terrible we feel when we hurt someone we love! We would do anything to make amends for the disappointment and heartbreak we have caused the beloved. Let us not grieve the indwelling Holy Spirit, who is the source of love in us. May we rather "be filled with the Spirit" (Eph. 5:18).

D.L. Moody related this experience of the fullness of the Spirit in his life to E.J. Goodspeed, author of a Moody-Sankey history published in 1876:

One day in New York, oh, what a day, I cannot describe it; I seldom refer to it; it is almost too sacred an experience to name; I can only say God revealed Himself to me. I had such an experience of His love that I had to ask Him to stay His hand. I went to preaching again; the sermons were no different; I did not present any new truth; yet hundreds were converted, and I would not be placed back where I was before that blessed experience if you would give me all Glasgow.

Moody had such a great hunger and thirst after God's fullness that he searched—yes, even pleaded—for God to fill him. Do you really hunger and thirst for this love?

Step Five

We must begin to love by faith and believe God for the love we cannot muster in ourselves. We must say, "Lord, by faith I *will* love that unlovable person."

Some people are extremely difficult to love. Recently, a 22-year-old woman came to me for counsel. As we talked, she poured out a story of hate and bitterness toward her parents.

After reading to her from God's Word, I was able to lead her to accept Christ as her personal Saviour. Almost immediately she said, "I want to be reconciled with my parents, but how can I love them?"

"By faith," I replied. "Go home and believe that God will give you a new love for your mother and father."

How can you love? Think of someone who gets on your nerves. Make a list of that person's good qualities and his objectionable qualities. You might then ask why he has those undesirable qualities. Then, in an act of genuine faith, resolve to love that person. Pray for him. Ask God to bless him. Prayer has a boomerang effect; it benefits the one who prays. Remember, it was when Job prayed for his miserable comforters that he was released from his own captivity.

Just as we accept new life by faith in Christ, we are to accept by faith the fullness of the Spirit, which He promises us. Paul, writing to the Galatians, stated that Christ redeemed us so "that we might receive the promise of the Spirit through faith" (3:14). Because it is "through faith," this gift is within reach of every believer. The youngest Christian can understand and know that fullness of love.

We must not look at ourselves and our shortcomings and become depressed and bogged down. The disciples saw the hopelessness of living a life of love by their own strength. They knew it was impossible, and so do we. But the great good news is just this: God knows it too! Let us look at Jesus Christ and His faithfulness. God's perfect character stands behind His promises. His perfect love will fill us if we let it. We need not struggle—but believe!

I have seen many learn how to love by taking these five basic steps. Will you learn how to love?

Love Lost and Found 12

"I have somewhat against thee, because thou hast left thy first love".
Rev. 2:4

Edmund Burke, in one of his speeches on English politics, describes the decline of character in a civil statesman. He says, "The instances are exceedingly rare of men immediately passing over a clear marked line from virtue into declared vice and corruption. There are middle tints and shades between the two extremes; there is something uncertain on the confines of the two empires which they must pass through, and which renders the change easy and imperceptible."

This is often true in the spiritual realm as well. Samson exposed himself to evil until a moral blindness made him oblivious to God's absence: "And he [knew] not that the Lord was departed from him" (Jud. 16:20). The early days of King Saul were like a magnificent sunrise; only gradually did the clouds appear, until blackness triumphed, and out of God's favor, he crawled off to consult the witch of Endor (1 Sam. 28:6-8).

The Ephesian believers were rebuked because they left their first love. Once these Christians were industrious, God-fearing, truth-abiding people, but they lost their original drive and devotion to the Lord. "I have somewhat against thee, because thou hast left thy first love" (Rev. 2:4). History tells us that this desertion continued until the Ephesian church died.

What Is "First Love"?

First love is the love we knew when we were converted. It is that exciting flood of response that we experienced when God assured us, "As far as the east is from the west, so far hath He removed our transgressions from us" (Ps. 103:12).

> This "first love" seeks not people, but a Person, the One who alone merits our *first* love. The "first love" is the intimate personal relationship of love which one has with our Lord Jesus Christ (M. Basilea Schlink, *Those Who Love Him*, Zondervan, p. 8).

First love is the total trust and the warm affection of the spiritually newborn person. First love looks at the grand possibilities rather than at the weight of the problems. To cross each river is a stirring challenge; to climb each mountain is an adventure. Stumbling stones become stepping-stones. Every obstacle is a fresh way to prove the omnipotence of God. First love is warm, radiant, and real.

Because it seeks first a *Person*, that Person empowers it to reach out to *people*. With wide-open arms, first love welcomes the world to its heart. It wears working clothes in the marketplace; it gets in touch with real people who have deep needs. First love is clean, expectant, strong, and involved.

The Apostle Paul knew this kind of love firsthand. Besides possessing a brilliant mind, he was endowed with a loving heart. His soul was a furnace of concern for his generation. Writing to the people of Rome, he said, "I am debtor both to the Greeks, and to the barbarians: both to the wise, and to the unwise" (Rom. 1:14). To the Thessalonian church he wrote, "For ye remember, brethren, our labor and travail; for laboring night and day, because we would not be chargeable unto any of you, we preached unto you the Gospel of God" (1 Thes. 2:9).

The word "travail" in 1 Thessalonians 2:9 indicates a deep concern, a struggle, even pain. Day and night Paul labored to fulfill his debt to his generation. I can hear him say, "I have a debt; I have an obligation; I must share the Gospel." To experience the real fruit of salvation is to love people. Personal salvation and loving people should be synonymous. To remain self-centered and silent in the light of salvation is to become some sort of monster. "No one can live without being a debtor; no one should live without being a creditor," wrote N.J. Panin.

One of the faces of love is a willingness to be involved in another person's pain. And if you are thus involved, you are going to suffer along with the one who is troubled. Loving is not easy and not free of hurt.

We human beings are constructed in a very complex way. It is our natural tendency to avoid pain or discomfort. We are masters at building protective devices into our lives. When we are rejected by another person, we almost automatically figure out how we can avoid that kind of hurt again. When someone screams at us or spits out some spiteful comment, our natural reaction is to protect our self-image by talking back or screaming louder. We are exceedingly clever at defending ourselves from hurt, from pain, from discomfort. Only as we keep pouring the love of God into the big, demanding hole of self are we prepared to take on the pain, the travail, that Paul talked about.

The intensity of Paul's involvement with others is reflected in his words to the church at Rome: "I have great heaviness and continual sorrow in my heart. For I could wish that myself were accursed from Christ for my brethren, my kinsmen according to the flesh" (Rom. 9:2-3). This is redemptive love. In plain talk, Paul is saying, "I am prepared to go to hell, if by so doing my friends and countrymen would believe in the Gospel." Isn't that staggering? That kind of love is difficult to comprehend.

That same spirit possessed Moses when he interceded for Israel. Moses prayed, "Oh, this people have sinned a great sin, and have made them gods of gold. Yet now, if Thou wilt forgive their sin—; and if not, blot me, I pray Thee, out of Thy book which Thou hast written" (Ex. 32:31–32). What love! What identification! Both Moses and Paul were possessed by supernatural love.

The Ephesian believers were hard working, patient, persevering, and thoroughly orthodox. The Lord, through the Apostle John, commended them for their many virtues (Rev. 2:2-3). The Christ of the candlesticks is not blind to the beauties of His people. He loves us, and He cares for us. He desires to see our lights burning brightly. In spite of the outstanding virtues of the Ephesian church, the Lord of the lampstands could tell that their love had declined into a noisy, pharisaic busyness. With the pain of wounded love He called, "I have somewhat against thee" (Rev. 2:4).

How Is First Love Lost?

First love is often lost because of sin! "Because iniquity shall abound, the love of many shall wax cold" (Matt. 24:12). Centuries ago Isaiah said, "Your iniquities have separated between you and your God, and your sins have hid His face from you, that He will not hear" (Isa. 59:2).

Sin is an obstacle to first love. It appears in two main forms—open rebellion against God, and a neglect of obedience to the revealed will of God.

Sin dulls first love. It builds a wall of separation between man and God. It darkens the lights of our life and blurs our understanding of the mind of God. Sin sears the conscience and drains our spiritual power.

A seared conscience is one whose warning voice has been suppressed and perverted habitually, so that eventually instead of serving as a guide, it only confirms the person in his premeditatedly evil course (Robert J. Little).

I heard a story once of an American eagle soaring magnificently into the sky. Suddenly it faltered, stopped, and plunged toward the earth, dead. Examination of the eagle showed that a small weasel had dug its claws into the abdomen of the bird, risen with the eagle into the sky, and drained the lifeblood while the eagle tried to escape. Sin behaves in a similar manner. It robs us of power and of life itself. If we take a friendly attitude toward sin, then Christ must take harsh measures with us.

Jesus sets before us a bold, unvarnished question:

Are you a bride or a whore? The two possibilities are related: it is only possible to become a whore because God has called us to be a bride. The call to love God creates the alternative, that we squander our love faithlessly. Jesus looks to us for the love of a bride. Any other love which possesses our heart brings us into the state of spiritual adultery (Schlink, *Those Who Love Him*, pp. 41-42).

Worldly concerns also detract from first love. One of the prevailing problems of the church today is the obsession to be accepted by society. Sophistication has all but smothered first love. The church is on an intellectual binge that is obscuring the effect of the Cross. We have become too concerned about what people will think. Sometimes we Christians are so tactful that we don't make contact.

Paul, with all his brilliance, would not permit the wisdom of this world to override the power of the Gospel. "For the preaching of the Cross is to them that perish foolishness; but unto us which are saved it is the power of God" (1 Cor. 1:18). Concern for what others might think has a chilling effect on first love, and Paul would not allow that kind of concern to sway him.

We may also lose the love we first knew by trying to enshrine it and isolate it, failing to let it bubble up through all of our relationships and experiences; or conversely, by gradually letting it go in the face of all the other demands on our attention.

Perhaps the clearest way to illustrate these twin dangers is to draw a parallel between first love and marital love. The first stage of a marriage relationship is that overwhelming experience of falling in love. Our love is so urgent, so total, that we stand alone with our beloved as though there were no one else in all the world. We want to share ourselves with no one else. We want to retain the flame, the intensity, that one-and-only feeling forever. So we marry—for keeps. But soon we begin to discover that the world is still with us after all. We are not two people isolated in a miraculous vacuum of love. We are a bit surprised to learn that we still have parents and in-laws, brothers and sisters, business associates and neighbors, old friends and strangers at the door. Somehow we have to begin to make room for all of these presences in our new life together.

It takes time. It takes arguments and tears. Those other people make unwanted demands on our marriage relationship. But we either learn how to keep our love warm and alive, while accommodating other people, or we get drawn into a complex network and pulled away from our loved one. People, appointments, work, and a thousand other things begin to pry us apart. Before we know it, the separation is almost unbridgeable. We look back across the gulf and say, "She's not the same person I married. We have so little in common. We really aren't compatible at all."

Is it possible that our love for Christ fails in this same way as we begin to get involved in service? As we stand back and look at this revolutionary love that has demanded total commitment of us, what do we see? Have we become so preoccupied with going to meetings, sounding good when we pray out loud working with church committees or organizations, meeting the local standards of church behavior, watching our own piety become noticeable to others, that we have lost sight of—don't have time for—the great Lover who first won us?

I came to see that my relationship to my Lord Jesus Christ, with the passing years, had eroded away something like a marriage gone humdrum. What did I do when I found a little pocket of spare time, on a Sunday or a holiday? I couldn't wait to get together with other people—people I liked, people with whom I had something in common—so we could share ideas and experiences. Or I read a stimulating book. Or I went out to enjoy nature. I even plunged further into my work, doing things that I normally didn't have time for. But to go to Jesus—to give Him first claim on even my spare time—that I did not do (Schlink, *Those Who Love Him*, pp. 8-9).

What happens as *you* begin to integrate your first love for Christ into your home life, your marriage, your office routine, your shop conversations, your school work? Do you stay in tune with that wondrous love that won you, and let the Holy Spirit show you how to share this freshness with others? Or do you hug it to yourself for fear of losing it, for fear of failing? Or do you become so busy with your chores, your deadlines, your concern with what others think, that you lose touch with the Holy Spirit and wonder if the experience was ever real in the first place?

How Is First Love Restored?

The big, and very practical, question is, How is first love restored?

The first step is to *remember*. The Lord is always found exactly where you left Him. He calls out, "Remember . . . from whence thou art fallen" (Rev. 2:5). Remember when you enjoyed the presence of God in everyday living? Can you recall the moments of satisfying communion in prayer? Remember when the hymns of the church rang often in your mind through the day's work? Remember when you wept, unashamedly and joyously, out of gratitude to Jesus for His goodness in your life? Remember when you sought out loved ones and friends to tell them what Jesus was doing for you?

Let us be glad and rejoice, and give honor to Him, for the marriage of the Lamb is come, and His wife hath made herself ready. And to her was granted that she should be arrayed in fine linen, clean and white, for the fine linen is the righteousness of saints (Rev. 19:7-8).

The second step is to *repent* and confess our sin. Holy memories should lead to holy action. The message of repentance has been nearly forgotten in our day. To repent means to turn around. It involves a change of mind, attitude, and conduct. It means to go back, simply and humbly, and start all over.

David, the man after God's own heart, enjoyed thrilling companionship with God. Yet during many careless periods of life, he went his own way. He saw a woman he wanted; he saw leadership he wanted; he saw power and status, and he connived to get what he wanted. The flesh asserted itself in all its ugliness. God said no, but David said yes and sinned greatly.

The Scriptures ask, "Can two walk together, except they be agreed?" (Amos 3:3) The answer is, emphatically, *no*. When David walked after his own desires, he walked without God. Many people think they are walking with God when actually they have walked off and left Him, because they are living contrary to God's Word. Whenever David sinned, though, the glad day of repentance always dawned, and he would cry, "Against Thee, Thee only, have I sinned, and done this evil in Thy sight" (Ps. 51:4). Each time David confessed his sin, immediately fellowship was restored, and God and David walked together once more. To confess means to say what God has said, to agree with God. David said, "Lord, I'm wrong, and You are right." That is confession. "Man is born with his back toward God. When he truly repents, he turns right around and faces God," said D.L. Moody.

The third step is to *return*. Repentance results in a return in conduct to what Jesus calls "first works" (Rev. 2:5).

What does He mean by "first works"? Surely this means daily fellowship with God. "First works" also means being mastered by the needs about us and serving others in a spontaneous sharing of the things of God. First works are not stingy but generous. The redemptive Word, which we take in our daily fellowship with God, issues forth in a redemptive work to others. The world outside the church is weary of listening to us talk without experiencing the concrete manifestations of our love. God's Holy Spirit can empower us to live and act as loudly as we talk. "First works" is the twin of "first love"; positive action, moving out of our own preoccupations to care for other people, demonstrates our love for Jesus Christ. If this seems very difficult, try praying specifically for someone you want to care about. Prayer often leads to love.

The Apostle John concludes his message to Ephesus with a severe warning from the Lord: "I will come unto thee quickly, and will remove thy candlestick out of his place, except thou repent" (Rev. 2:5). For the church of Ephesus, it was either revival or removal. Sadly, the Ephesians refused the message of John, and they suffered the consequences. They were removed!

I have known Christians personally who have been removed

by God, apparently because they refused to heed His rebuke. In New Testament times, Ananias and Sapphira were removed when they persisted in living a lie (Acts 5:1-10). To the Corinthians, who participated carelessly in the ordinance of the Lord's table, Paul wrote, "For this cause many are weak and sickly among you, and many sleep" (1 Cor. 11:30). Some of the Corinthians were removed because they refused to change their ways.

Where is Ephesus today? Where is the light that once burned so brightly? The light is long gone, and the church of Ephesus exists no more.

God's message to us today is just the same as it was to these believers of the first century: remember, repent, and return! "Beloved," says Jude, "keep yourselves in the love of God" (vv. 20-21). What less can we ask today?

Appendix
Selected Scripture
Portions on Love

And thou shalt love the Lord Thy God with all Thine heart, and with all Thy soul, and with all Thy might (Deut. 6:5).

The Lord did not set His love upon you, nor choose you, because ye were more in number than any people; for ye were the fewest of all people. But because the Lord loved you, and because He would keep the oath which He had sworn unto your fathers, hath the Lord brought you out with a mighty hand, and redeemed you out of the house of bondage, from the hand of Pharaoh king of Egypt (Deut. 7:7-8).

Oh, love the Lord, all ye His saints; for the Lord preserveth the faithful, and plentifully rewardeth the proud doer (Ps. 31:23).

A friend loveth at all times, and a brother is born for adversity (Prov. 17:17).

Set me as a seal upon Thine heart, as a seal upon thine arm, for love is strong as death, jealousy is cruel as the grave; the coals thereof are coals of fire, which hath a most vehement flame. Many waters cannot quench love, neither can the floods drown it. If a man would give all the substance of his house for love, it would utterly be [rejected] (Song of Sol. 8:6-7).

The Lord hath appeared of old unto me, saying, "Yea, I have loved thee with an everlasting love; therefore, with loving-kindness have I drawn thee" (Jer. 31:3).

Ye have heard that it hath been said, "Thou shalt love thy neighbor, and hate thine enemy"; but I say unto you, Love your enemies, bless them that curse you, do good to them that hate you, and pray for them who despitefully use you, and persecute you; that ye may be the sons of your Father, who is in heaven; for He maketh His sun to rise on the evil and on the good, and sendeth rain on the just and on the unjust. For if ye love them who love you, what reward have ye? Do not even the publicans [tax collectors] the same? And if ye salute [greet] your brethren only, what do ye more than others? Do not even the publicans so? Be ye, therefore, perfect, even as your Father, who is in heaven, is perfect (Matt. 5:43-48).

Jesus said unto him, "Thou shalt love the Lord thy God with all thy heart, and with all thy soul, and with all thy mind. This is the first and great commandment. And the second is like unto it. Thou shalt love thy neighbor as thyself. On these two commandments hang all the Law and the Prophets" (Matt. 22:37-40).

But I say unto you [that] hear, Love your enemies, do good to them who hate you, bless them that curse you, and pray for them who despitefully use you (Luke 6:27-28).

Wherefore I say unto thee, Her sins, which are many, are forgiven; for she loved much. But to whom little is forgiven, the same loveth little (Luke 7:47).

And, behold, a certain lawyer stood up, and tempted [tested] Him, saying, "Master, what shall I do to inherit eternal life?" He said unto him, "What is written in the Law? How readest thou?" And he, answering, said, "'Thou shalt love the Lord thy God with all thy heart, and with all thy soul, and with all thy strength, and with all thy mind; and thy neighbor as thyself.'" And He said unto him, "Thou hast answered right; this do, and thou shalt live." But he, willing [desiring] to justify himself, said unto Jesus, "And who is my neighbor?" And Jesus, answering said, "A certain man went down from Jerusalem to Jericho, and fell among thieves, [who] stripped him of his raiment, and wounded him, and departed, leaving him half dead. And by chance there came down a certain priest that way; and when he saw him, he passed by on the other side. And likewise a Levite, when he was at the place, came and looked on him, and passed by on the other side. But a certain Samaritan, as he journeyed, came where he was; and when he saw him, he had compassion on him, and went to him, and bound up his wounds, pouring in oil and wine, and set him on his own beast, and brought him to an inn, and took care of him. And on the morrow, when he departed, he took out two pence [denarii], and gave them to the host, and said unto him, 'Take care of him; and whatever thou spendest more, when I come again, I will repay thee.' Which now, of these three, thinkest thou, was neighbor unto him that fell among the thieves?" And he said, "He that showed mercy on him." Then said Jesus unto him, "Go, and do thou likewise" (Luke 10:25-37).

If ye love Me, keep My commandments. And I will pray the Father, and He shall give you another Comforter, that He may abide with you forever. . . . He that hath My commandments, and keepeth them, he it is that loveth Me; and he that loveth Me shall be loved of My Father, and I will love him, and will manifest Myself to him (John 14:15-16, 21).

As the Father hath loved Me, so have I loved you; continue ye in My love. If ye keep My commandments, ye shall abide in My love, even as I have kept My Father's commandments, and abide in His love. These things have I spoken unto you, that My joy might remain in you, and that your joy might be full. This is My commandment, that ye love one another, as I have loved you. Greater love hath no man than this, that a man lay down his life for his friends. Ye are My friends, if ye do whatever I command you (John 15:9-14).

So when they had dined, Jesus saith to Simon Peter, "Simon, son of Jonah, lovest thou Me more than these?" He saith unto him, "Yea, Lord; Thou knowest that I love Thee." He saith unto him, "Feed My lambs." He saith to him again the second time, "Simon, son of Jonah, lovest thou Me?" He saith unto Him, "Yea, Lord; thou knowest that I love Thee." He saith unto him, "Feed My sheep" (John 21:15-16).

And hope maketh not ashamed, because the love of God is shed abroad in our hearts by the Holy Spirit [who] is given unto us (Rom. 5:5).

But God commendeth His love toward us, in that, while we were yet sinners, Christ died for us (Rom. 5:8).

And we know that all things work together for good to them that love God, to them who are the called according to His purpose. . . . Who shall separate us from the love of Christ? Shall tribulation, or distress, or persecution, or famine, or nakedness, or peril, or sword? As it is written, "For Thy sake we are killed all the day long; we are accounted as sheep for the slaughter." Nay, in all these things we are more than conquerors through Him that loved us. For I am persuaded that neither death, nor life, nor angels, nor principalities, nor powers, nor things present, nor things to come, nor height, nor depth, nor any other creature, shall be able to separate us from the love of God, which is in Christ Jesus, our Lord (Rom. 8:28, 35-39).

Let love be without dissimulation [hypocrisy]. Abhor that which is evil; cleave to that which is good. Be kindly affectioned one to another with brotherly love, in honor preferring one another (Rom. 12:9-10).

Owe no man any thing, but to love one another; for he that loveth another hath fulfilled the Law. For this, Thou shalt not commit adultery, Thou shalt not kill, "Thou shalt not steal, Thou shalt not bear false witness, Thou shalt not covet" and if there be any other commandment, it is briefly comprehended in this saying, namely, Thou shalt love thy neighbor as thyself. Love worketh no ill to its neighbor; therefore, love is the fulfilling of the Law (Rom. 13:8-10).

Now as touching things offered unto idols, we know that we all have knowledge. Knowledge puffeth up, but [love] edifieth. And if any man think that he knoweth anything, he knoweth noth-

ing yet as he ought to know. But if any man love God, the same is known of him (1 Cor. 8:1-3).

But if any have caused grief, he hath not grieved me, but in part: that I may not overcharge [burden] you all. Sufficient to such a man is this punishment, which was inflicted by the many. So that contrariwise ye ought rather to forgive him, and comfort him, lest perhaps such a one should be swallowed up with overmuch sorrow. Wherefore, I beseech you that ye would confirm your love toward him (2 Cor. 2:5-8).

Behold, the third time I am ready to come to you; and I will not be burdensome to you, for I seek not yours, but you. For the children ought not to lay up for the parents, but the parents for the children. And I will very gladly spend and be spent for you; though the more abundantly I love you, the less I be loved (2 Cor. 12:14-15).

But the fruit of the Spirit is love, joy, peace, long-suffering, gentleness, goodness, faith, meekness, self-control; against such there is no law (Gal. 5:22-23).

Having predestinated us unto the adoption of children by Jesus Christ to Himself, according to the good pleasure of His will, to the praise of the glory of His grace, wherein He hath made us accepted in the beloved. In whom we have redemption through His blood, the forgiveness of sins, according to the riches of His grace (Eph. 1:5-7).

But God, who is rich in mercy, for His great love wherewith He loved us, even when we were dead in sins, hath quickened [made us alive] together with Christ (by grace ye are saved), and hath raised us up together, and made us sit together in heavenly places in Christ Jesus. . . . Not of works, lest any man should boast (Eph. 2:4-6, 9).

That Christ may dwell in your hearts by faith; that ye, being rooted and grounded in love, may be able to comprehend, with all saints, what is the breadth, and length, and depth, and height, and to know the love of Christ, which passeth knowledge, that ye might be filled with all the fullness of God (Eph. 3:17-19).

With all lowliness and meekness, with long-suffering, forbearing one another in love (Eph. 4:2).

That we henceforth be no more children, tossed to and fro, and carried about with every wind of doctrine, by the sleight of men, and cunning craftiness, by which they lie in wait to deceive; but, speaking the truth in love, may grow up into Him in all things, [who] is the head, even Christ (Eph. 4:14-15).

And this I pray, that your love may abound yet more and more in knowledge and in all judgment (Phil. 1:9).

That their hearts might be comforted, being knit together in love and unto all riches of the full assurance of understanding, to the acknowledgment of the mystery of God, and of the Father, and of Christ (Col. 2:2).

Wives, submit yourselves unto your own husbands, as it is fit in the Lord. Husbands, love your wives, and be not bitter against them. Children, obey your parents in all things; for this is well pleasing unto the Lord (Col. 3:18-20).

So, being affectionately desirous of you, we were willing to have imparted unto you, not the Gospel of God only but also our own souls, because ye were dear unto us (1 Thes. 2:8).

But as touching brotherly love ye need not that I write unto you: for ye yourselves are taught of God to love one another. And indeed ye do it toward all the brethren who are in all Macedonia. But we beseech you, brethren, that ye increase more and more, and that ye study to be quiet, and to do your own business, and to work with your own hands, as we commanded you (1 Thes. 4:9-11).

But we are bound to give thanks always to God for you, brethren beloved of the Lord, because God hath from the beginning chosen you to salvation through sanctification of the Spirit and belief of the truth (2 Thes. 2:13).

Now the end of the commandment is [love] out of a pure heart, and of a good conscience, and of faith unfeigned (1 Tim. 1:5).

And the grace of our Lord was exceedingly abundant with faith and love which is in Christ Jesus (1 Tim. 1:14).

For God hath not given us the spirit of fear, but of power, and of love, and of a sound mind (2 Tim. 1:7).

Flee also youthful lusts, but follow righteousness, faith, [love], peace, with them that call on the Lord out of a pure heart (2 Tim. 2:22).

Let brotherly love continue. Be not forgetful to entertain strangers; for thereby some have entertained angels unawares (Heb. 13:1-2).

Seeing ye have purified your souls in obeying the truth through the Spirit unto unfeigned love of the brethren, see that ye love one another with a pure heart fervently (1 Peter 1:22).

Finally, be ye all of one mind, having compassion one of another, love as brethren, be pitiful, be courteous, not rendering evil for evil, or railing for railing, but contrariwise blessing, knowing that ye are called to this, that ye should inherit a blessing (1 Peter 3:8-9).

And above all things have fervent [love] among yourselves; for love shall cover the multitude of sins. Use hospitality one to another without grudging. As every man hath received the gift, even so minister the same one to another, as good stewards of the manifold grace of God (1 Peter 4:8-10).

Simon Peter, a servant and an apostle of Jesus Christ, to them that have obtained like precious faith with us through the righteousness of God and our Saviour, Jesus Christ: Grace and peace be multiplied unto you through the knowledge of God, and of Jesus, our Lord, according as His divine power hath given unto us all things that pertain unto life and godliness, through the knowledge of Him that hath called us to glory and virtue; by which are given unto us exceedingly great and precious promises, that by these ye might be partakers of the divine nature, having escaped the corruption that is in the world through lust. And beside this, giving all diligence, add to your faith virtue; and to virtue, knowledge; and to knowledge, temperance [self-control]; and to [self-control], patience; and to patience, godliness; and to godliness, brotherly kindness; and to brotherly kindness [love] (2 Peter 1:1-7).

And by this we do know that we know Him, if we keep His commandments. He that saith, I know Him, and keepeth not His commandments, is a liar, and the truth is not in him. But whosoever keepeth His Word, in him verily is the love of God perfected; [hereby] know we that we are in Him. He that saith he abideth in Him ought himself also so to walk, even as He walked (1 John 2:3-6).

We know that we have passed from death unto life, because we love the brethren. He that loveth not his brother abideth in death. Whosoever hateth his brother is a murderer; and ye know that no murderer hath eternal life abiding in him. [Hereby] perceive we the love of God, because He laid down His life for us; and we ought to lay down our lives for the brethren. But whoso hath this world's good, and seeth his brother have need, and shutteth up his compassions from him, how dwelleth the love of God in him? My little children, let us not love in word, neither in tongue, but in deed and in truth (1 John 3:14-18).

Beloved, if God so loved us, we ought also to love one another. No man hath seen God at any time. If we love one another, God dwelleth in us, and His love is perfected in us. . . . There is no fear in love, but perfect love casteth out fear, because fear hath punishment (1 John 4:11-12, 18).

Keep yourselves in the love of God, looking for the mercy of our Lord Jesus Christ unto eternal life (Jude 21).

Unto the angel of the church of Ephesus write: These things saith He that holdeth the seven stars in His right hand, who walketh in the midst of the seven golden candlesticks [lampstands]. "I know thy works, and thy labor, and thy patience, and how thou canst not bear them who are evil; and thou hast tried them who say they are apostles, and are not, and hast found them liars; and hast borne, and hast patience, and for My name's sake hast labored, and hast not fainted. Nevertheless, I have somewhat against thee, because thou hast left thy first love. Remember, therefore, from where thou art fallen, and repent, and do the first works, or else I will come unto thee quickly, and will remove thy [lampstand] out of [its] place, except thou repent" (Rev. 2:1-5).